REGENTS RESTORATION DR

General Editor: John Loftis

LUCIUS JUNIUS BRUTUS

NATHANIEL LEE

Lucius Junius Brutus

Edited by

JOHN LOFTIS

UNIVERSITY OF NEBRASKA PRESS · LINCOLN

Publishers on the Plains

UNP

MANUFACTURED IN THE UNITED STATES OF AMERICA

Regents Restoration Drama Series

The Regents Restoration Drama Series provides soundly edited texts, in modern spellings, of the more significant plays of the late seventeenth and early eighteenth centuries. The word "Restoration" is here used ambiguously and must be explained. If to the historian it refers to the period between 1660 and 1685 (or 1688), it has long been used by the student of the drama in default of a more precise word to refer to plays belonging to the dramatic tradition established in the 1660's, weakening after 1700, and displaced in the 1730's. It is in this extended sense—imprecise though justified by academic custom—that the word is used in this series, which includes plays first produced between 1660 and 1737. Although these limiting dates are determined by political events, the return of Charles II (and the removal of prohibitions against the operation of theaters) and the passage of Walpole's Stage Licensing Act, they enclose a period of dramatic history having a coherence of its own in the establishment, development, and disintegration of a tradition.

Some fifteen editions having appeared as this volume goes to press, the series has reached perhaps a third of its anticipated range of between forty and fifty volumes. The volumes will continue to be published for a number of years, at the rate of three or more annually. From the beginning the editors have planned the series with attention to the projected dimensions of the completed whole, a representative collection of Restoration drama providing a record of artistic achievement and providing also a record of the deepest concerns of three generations of Englishmen. And thus it contains deservedly famous plays—*The Country Wife*, *The Man of Mode*, and *The Way of the World*—and also significant but little known plays, *The Virtuoso*, for example, and *City Politiques*, the former a satirical review of scientific investigation in the early years of the Royal Society, the latter an equally satirical review of politics at the time of the Popish Plot. If the volumes of famous plays finally achieve the larger circulation, the other volumes may conceivably have the greater utility, in making available texts otherwise difficult of access with the editorial apparatus needed to make them intelligible.

The editors have had the instructive example of the parallel and senior project, the Regents Renaissance Drama Series; they have in fact used the editorial policies developed for the earlier plays as their own, modifying them as appropriate for the later period and as the experience of successive editions suggested. The introductions to the separate Restoration plays differ considerably in their nature. Although a uniform body of relevant information is presented in each of them, no attempt has been made to impose a pattern of interpretation. Emphasis in the introductions has necessarily varied with the nature of the plays and inevitably—we think desirably—with the special interests and aptitudes of the different editors.

Each text in the series is based on a fresh collation of the seventeenth- and eighteenth-century editions that might be presumed to have authority. The textual notes, which appear above the rule at the bottom of each page, record all substantive departures from the edition used as the copy-text. Variant substantive readings among contemporary editions are listed there as well. Editions later than the eighteenth century are referred to in the textual notes only when an emendation originating in some one of them is received into the text. Variants of accidentals (spelling, punctuation, capitalization) are not recorded in the notes. Contracted forms of characters' names are silently expanded in speech prefixes and stage directions, and, in the case of speech prefixes, are regularized. Additions to the stage directions of the copy-text are enclosed in brackets.

Spelling has been modernized along consciously conservative lines, but within the limits of a modernized text the linguistic quality of the original has been carefully preserved. Contracted preterites have regularly been expanded. Punctuation has been brought into accord with modern practices. The objective has been to achieve a balance between the pointing of the old editions and a system of punctuation which, without overloading the text with exclamation marks, semicolons, and dashes, will make the often loosely flowing verse and prose of the original syntactically intelligible to the modern reader. Dashes are regularly used only to indicate interrupted speeches, or shifts of address within a single speech.

Explanatory notes, chiefly concerned with glossing obsolete words and phrases, are printed below the textual notes at the bottom of each page. References to stage directions in the notes follow the admirable system of the Revels editions, whereby stage directions are keyed, decimally, to the line of the text before or after which they occur.

Thus, a note on 0.2 has reference to the second line of the stage direction at the beginning of the scene in question. A note on 115.1 has reference to the first line of the stage direction following line 115 of the text of the relevant scene. Speech prefixes, and any stage directions attached to them, are keyed to the first line of accompanying dialogue.

JOHN LOFTIS

October, 1967
Stanford University

Contents

List of Abbreviations

C1	Collected works, 1713
C2	Collected works, 1722
C3	Collected works, 1734
OED	*Oxford English Dictionary*
om.	omitted
Q1	First quarto, 1681
Q2	Second quarto, 1708
S-C	*The Works of Nathaniel Lee*, ed. Thomas B. Stroup and Arthur L. Cooke (New Brunswick, N.J.: The Scarecrow Press, 1954, 1955).
S.D.	stage direction
S.P.	speech prefix

Introduction

The first edition of *Lucius Junius Brutus* (Q1), the only one to appear in Lee's lifetime, is a quarto printed for Richard and Jacob Tonson in 1681: it was recorded in *The Term Catalogues* for Trinity Term (June) of that year.[1] The play was carelessly printed, though most of the typographical errors are obvious ones that do not create ambiguities. A second quarto (Q2), printed for J. T. and sold by R. Wellington in 1708, is for the most part a page-by-page reprint of Q1: except for the preliminaries the pagination is followed exactly until page 66. Q2 follows the text of Q1 closely, even to reproducing some obvious errors, though it corrects a number of misprints. The play appears in three early eighteenth-century collected editions of Lee's works: those printed in 1713 for R. Wellington (C1), in 1722 for M. P. and Sam. Chapman (C2), and in 1734 for W. Feales and others (C3). C1 usually follows Q2 though occasionally Q1; the compositor had access to both, and he corrected errors in them. The accidentals in this as in the two subsequent collected editions are to some extent normalized; and all three of these editions are carefully printed. C2 was set from C1, and C3 from C2. The play was reprinted several times during the eighteenth and nineteenth centuries; it is included in Bell's *British Theatre* in the late eighteenth century and, in this century, in the excellent edition of Lee's *Works* (S-C) by Thomas B. Stroup and Arthur L. Cooke (1954, 1955).

The present edition, in modern spelling, follows as copy-text a first quarto in the library of Professor Norman Philbrick. Two other copies of Q1, both in the Henry E. Huntington Library, have been compared with it, neither revealing any substantive variants. Q2 and C1 have been collated with Q1 and all substantive variants recorded in the textual notes. Where variants occur, the readings of C2 and C3 have also been recorded.

[1] Edward Arber, ed., *The Term Catalogues* (London, 1903), I, 451: "Trinity Term, 1681. [June] *Lucius Junius Brutus*, Father of his Country. A Tragedy, acted at the Duke's Theatre for six days; but then prohibited. Written by N. Lee. Quarto. Price 1s."

Although able critics have praised *Lucius Junius Brutus* warmly,[2] it had a very short original run, and it was never again performed in London (though it was revived briefly in Dublin in 1738, according to *The Dublin News-Letter*, April 22 to 25). Produced by the Duke's Company acting in the Dorset Garden Theatre early in December, 1680, it was presented only a few days before it was suppressed by the Lord Chamberlain. We know little about the production except what can be inferred from the names of the actors printed with their roles in the dramatis personae of the first edition. Thomas Betterton, then at the height of his powers, played Brutus, and he may be assumed to have given the role an appropriate dignity. His wife played Lucrece, and it is probably significant that a woman of her reputation for virtue should have had the part. Elizabeth Barry, appropriately enough for the actress who had earlier distinguished herself as Roxana in Lee's *The Rival Queens*, had the passionate role of Teraminta; and opposite her in the role of Titus was William Smith, one of the company's most accomplished actors. The comedian James Nokes had the part of Vinditius, a circumstance assuring us that the character (who, as will be argued below, is intended to represent Titus Oates) was portrayed in a broad and comic fashion. With actors of such talents performing in it, there is reason enough to believe the assertion made much later in *The Poetical Register* that the audience received the play "with great Applause." [3]

The Lord Chamberlain's order of suppression, dated December 11, 1680, cites the play's political offences: "Whereas I am informed that there is Acted by you a Play called Lucius Junius Brutus . . . wherein are very Scandalous Expressions & Reflections vpon ye Government these are to require you Not to Act ye said Play again." [4] Testimony as to how many days the play had run is conflicting. Charles Gildon, writing in 1703 in the preface to *The Patriot*, his adaptation of *Lucius Junius Brutus*, says that it was acted only three days before it was silenced "as an antimonarchical play, and wrote when the nation was in a ferment of Whig and Tory as a compliment to the former." Yet

---

[2] Cf. Roswell Gray Ham, *Otway and Lee* (New Haven, 1931), pp. 151–154; G. Wilson Knight, *The Golden Labyrinth* (New York, 1962), pp. 165–167.

[3] Giles Jacob, *The Poetical Register* (1719), I, 162 (cited in William Van Lennep, "The Life and Works of Nathaniel Lee; A Study of the Sources" [unpublished dissertation, Harvard University, 1933], p. 452).

[4] P.R.O., L.C. 5/144, p. 28 (quoted from Allardyce Nicoll, *A History of Restoration Drama*, 1660–1700, 4th ed. [Cambridge, 1952], p. 10 n.).

the entry for the play in *The Term Catalogues* says that it ran six days before it was prohibited, a statement supported by a manuscript note of William Oldys asserting that John Boman the actor told him it ran that long.[5] The stronger evidence would thus suggest six days.

Although *Lucius Junius Brutus* was never again acted in London, it provided the basis for an independent play, Gildon's *The Patriot* of 1703, which, despite the fact that its setting is Renaissance Italy, takes over half its lines from Lee.[6] Gildon explains in his preface that he first revised *Lucius Junius Brutus* by merely removing from it all passages reflecting on monarchy. When the Master of the Revels refused to license it, Gildon substituted Cosmo de Medici for Brutus as protagonist, a change made possible by a parallel between their careers, and this time the play was licensed, though even with its reduced political voltage Gildon took care to provide it with a prologue disclaiming anti-monarchical principles.

When *Lucius Junius Brutus* is read with knowledge of the political events of 1680, it is easy enough to understand why it was not permitted on the stage once its import was understood. Like other seventeenth-century Englishmen, Lee had looked to Roman history for illustration of his political beliefs, and he had found events he could reinterpret as a commentary on the English constitutional crisis precipitated by the Popish Plot. The play could scarcely have been permitted at any time during Charles II's reign, and least of all in December, 1680, two years after Titus Oates' allegations about a Jesuit plot to murder the king had plunged the nation into turmoil, a time when the fate of the Exclusion Bill had not yet been determined, only three months before the Oxford Parliament with its threat of revolution. Lee cannot have been unaware that he was writing anti-Catholic propaganda. His play is a part of the literature of the Popish Plot, containing, in the episodes of the conjuration against the new Roman republic, a loosely allegorical version of the Plot as it was envisioned by the Whigs.

The play is, by implication, a statement of the Whig constitutional position during the Exclusion controversy, the more significant because of its date, eight years before the Revolution and a decade

[5] MS. note in a copy of Gerard Langbaine, *An Account of the English Dramatick Poets* (1691), in the British Museum (cited in Van Lennep, p. 452).

[6] Thomas B. Stroup and Arthur L. Cooke, eds., *The Works of Nathaniel Lee* (New Brunswick, N.J.: The Scarecrow Press, 1954, 1955), II, 317.

before the publication of Locke's *Two Treatises on Government*. Lee's subject, Brutus' expulsion of Tarquin and the establishment of the Roman republic, was a precedent often cited in the seventeenth century by theorists who advocated a form of government with powers divided among a chief of state, an aristocracy, and the people; for many seventeenth-century theorists it provided, as modern scholarship has demonstrated, an example of the superiority of a "mixed" form of government (i.e., government in which there is a division of powers) over a "pure" form of government such as absolute monarchy.[7] In dramatizing the career of Brutus, Lee associated himself by implication with such seventeenth-century "classical republicans" as John Milton; and that he did so with knowledge of the relevant issues in political theory is implied by his allusion in his dedicatory epistle to Machiavelli's *Discorsi sopra la Prima Deca di Tito Livio*. Machiavelli was one of the most influential expositors of the classical theory—expressed by Polybius and Cicero, among others—of the instability of a pure form of government in contrast with the stability of a mixed government.[8]

A play about a revolution that had as its result the substitution of a republic for a monarchy, *Lucius Junius Brutus* is a celebration of constitutionalism; the king's violation of constitutional principles provides a justification for the revolution, in Lee as indeed earlier in the historians of Rome. Brutus accuses Tarquin, in his inflammatory speech over the dead body of Lucrece, of

> Invading fundamental right and justice,
> Breaking the ancient customs, statutes, laws,
> With positive power and arbitrary lust;
> And those affairs which were before dispatched
> In public by the fathers, now are forced
> To his own palace, there to be determined
> As he and his portentous council please.
> (II.i.179–185)

Livy had described Tarquin's violation of the senate's constitutional rights:

Hic enim regum primus traditum a prioribus morem de omnibus senatum consulendi solvit, domesticis consiliis rem publicam

---

[7] Zera S. Fink, *The Classical Republicans: An Essay in the Recovery of a Pattern of Thought in Seventeenth Century England* (Evanston, Ill., 1945), pp. 6–7.

[8] *Ibid.*, pp. 10–11; Leslie J. Walker, ed. and trans., *The Discourses of Niccolò Machiavelli* (New Haven, 1950), Introduction, I, 136–137.

administravit; bellum, pacem, foedera, societates per se ipse, cum quibus voluit, iniussu populi ac senatus, fecit diremitque. Latinorum sibi maxime gentem conciliabat, ut peregrinis quoque opibus tutior inter cives esset, neque hospitia modo cum primoribus eorum, sed adfinitates quoque iungebat. Octavio Mamilio Tusculano—is longe princeps Latini nominis erat, si famae credimus, ab Ulixe deaque Circa oriundus—ei Mamilio filiam nuptum dat perque eas nuptias multos sibi cognatos amicosque eius conciliat.[9]

No very lively imagination is required to see the relevance of all this to Stuart policy, to that of Charles I as well as that of Charles II, both of whom circumvented Parliament and cultivated a foreign power, France, by matrimonial alliance as well as by other means. At the time the play was performed, Charles II was receiving large subsidies from Louis XIV, which in limited measure freed him from dependence on Parliament.[10] The play repeatedly comments on constitutional issues. Brutus' exposition to the senate of the need for a monarch to limit himself by law has an inescapable application to Restoration politics:

> Laws, rules, and bounds, prescribed for raging kings,
> Like banks and bulwarks for the mother seas,
> Though 'tis impossible they should prevent
> A thousand daily wracks and nightly ruins,
> Yet help to break those rolling inundations
> Which else would overflow and drown the world.
>
> (III.ii.11–16)

[9] *Ab Urbe Condita* I.xlix.7–9, trans. B. O. Foster (Loeb Library), I, 172–173: "For this king was the first to break with the custom handed down by his predecessors, of consulting the senate on all occasions, and governed the nation without other advice than that of his own household. War, peace, treaties, and alliances were entered upon or broken off by the monarch himself, with whatever states he wished, and without the decree of people or senate. The Latin race he strove particularly to make his friends, that his strength abroad might contribute to his security at home. He contracted with their nobles not only relations of hospitality but also matrimonial connections. To Octavius Mamilius of Tusculum, a man by long odds the most important of the Latin name, and descended, if we may believe report, from Ulysses and the goddess Circe, he gave his daughter in marriage, and in this way attached to himself the numerous kinsmen and friends of the man."

[10] Cf. David Ogg, *England in the Reign of Charles II* (Oxford, 1963), II, 598–602.

INTRODUCTION

At a time when the Stuart conception of the royal prerogative was in dispute, a resounding declamation of such lines would have sounded like a Whig manifesto. In the absence of contemporary records, we may only guess at the excitement produced by Betterton's dignified and rhetorical delivery of them.

Lee's attack on the Catholics in *Lucius Junius Brutus* is blunt and direct. The conjuration, led by priests who employ a religious ritual resembling a Catholic mass to intimidate their superstitious followers, conveys some notion of the fears which haunted the Whigs during that troubled era. Tiberius' sadistic account, early in Act IV, of the conspirators' plans for taking over Rome sounds like a rendering of current talk about the Jesuits' plans for taking over London. The conspirators' objective is to overthrow a constitutional government and re-establish an absolute monarchy; their plans, as they are subsequently revealed in captured documents, resemble the alleged program of the Popish Plot:

> The sum of the conspiracy to the king.
> It shall begin with both the consuls' deaths,
> And then the senate; every man must bleed,
> But those that have engaged to serve the king.
>   (IV.i.255–258)

The plot is frustrated by a crafty and persistent informer, Vinditius (mentioned by both Plutarch and Livy), apparently representing Titus Oates, for the two resemble each other not only in the supposed service to their respective nations but also in their unamiable characteristics of self-importance and ambition. "Why, what, they'll make me a senator at least," says Vinditius (IV.i.218–219), "And then a consul," in what sounds like a satirical reference to Titus Oates' expectation of a bishopric. All this is enough to have satisfied that Restoration fondness for crypto-history to which Dryden appealed a few months later in his Tory poem *Absalom and Achitophel*.

The political theme of *Lucius Junius Brutus*, which points on the one hand back to the Interregnum, to Cromwell and John Milton, and on the other forward to the Revolution, to William III, Nicholas Rowe, and Joseph Addison, provides an illuminating contrast to that of Dryden's great political poem.[11] Dryden's frightened horror at mob violence is not unlike Lee's at royal tyranny. Dryden's emotional

[11] Cf. John Loftis, *The Politics of Drama in Augustan England* (Oxford, 1963). For discussion of the political theme of *Absalom and Achitophel*, see Bernard N. Schilling, *Dryden and the Conservative Myth* (New Haven, 1961).

veneration for monarchy would soon become obsolete; Lee's conception of constitutionalism in a government of divided powers would soon be generally accepted, though the anti-monarchical and republican implications of the play provided difficulties even after the Revolution. Thus, although we find Lee's play again forbidden in the first years of the eighteenth century, we encounter in the 1730's two more, though much inferior, dramatizations of Brutus' defiance of Tarquin, William Bond's *The Tuscan Treaty; Or, Tarquin's Overthrow* (Covent Garden, 1733) and William Duncombe's *Junius Brutus* (Drury Lane, 1734), and both of them point a political moral similar to Lee's. This political moral is all but inevitable in any sympathetic rendering of the story of Brutus, appearing to some extent even in Voltaire's French tragedy on the subject.

Even in Livy the story has political implications. Looking to the remote past, Livy found examples of antique Roman virtue and fortitude—Lucrece's resolution not to outlive the loss of her chastity; Brutus' subordination of paternal affection to the needs of the state— and he described them with a didactic purpose. Like his contemporaries Virgil and Horace he enjoyed the personal friendship of the Emperor Augustus, and like them he gave literary expression to political ideals the Emperor found congenial.[12] The veneration for Rome in her history that animates the first Decade of *Ab Urbe Condita*, it has been noted, resembles the veneration for the Roman past, quasi-religious in character, that permeates the *Aeneid*.[13] And thus the generations of Englishmen who liked to think of themselves as Augustans could find in Livy, especially in his first ten books, examples of idealized conduct that confirmed their conception of ancient Rome. Livy's Romans of the monarchy and early republic, above all, perhaps, Brutus, who bridged the two periods, provided for the English Augustans, as they had for the Romans who were Livy's contemporaries, classic examples of heroic virtue.

Here, in the adaptation and naturalization of a group of Roman heroes, is a major component of English "Augustanism." Insofar as the term was more than merely an evaluative one of self-congratulation, it implied an admiration for and an emulation of the personal and literary standards and achievements of Virgil and his contemporaries. In *Lucius Junius Brutus* Lee gives us one of the most satisfactory renderings of a Roman myth turned to English uses.

[12] Ronald Syme, *The Roman Revolution* (Oxford, 1960), pp. 317–318.
[13] P. G. Walsh, *Livy: His Historical Aims and Methods* (Cambridge, 1961), pp. 10–11.

Employing the historians as intermediaries, he takes on the ideological coloration of the Roman Augustan Age—and turns it to the service of the Whigs.

The vehement Whiggism of *Lucius Junius Brutus* notwithstanding, Lee's two later plays, *The Duke of Guise* (1682), in which he collaborated with Dryden, and *Constantine the Great* (about 1683), are Tory in bias. His early plays had been largely free of politics, at most glancing in innuendo at the licentiousness of Charles II. But in *Caesar Borgia* of 1679 he had taken as subject a notorious despot, using him in an arraignment of Catholicism and tyranny alike, and this during the excitement over the Popish Plot; and probably it was at about the same time that he wrote the dramatization of the St. Bartholomew's Day massacre, *The Massacre of Paris*, which was not permitted on the stage during Charles' reign. His conversion to the Tory position in 1682 thus represented a complete change in his political allegiance. Perhaps he was influenced by his friend and collaborator Dryden, who also moved in a conservative direction; perhaps both of them merely changed with the nation, which during 1681 experienced a revulsion from Whig extremism. In any event *The Duke of Guise* resembles Dryden's *Absalom and Achitophel* in its political theme, with sixteenth-century France rather than ancient Israel providing the vehicle for allegory: the title character, an unprincipled political adventurer, represents the Whig candidate for succession, the Duke of Monmouth, and he is more harshly treated than is the Absalom of the poem. It was in the following year, 1683, so far as we can determine, that Lee wrote *Constantine the Great*, which includes an idealized rendering of a character representing the Duke of York and a condemnatory one of a character representing the Whig Earl of Shaftesbury.[14] All this is testimony to the completeness of the Tory victory.

Lucius Junius Brutus is less systematically allegorical than these two later plays, each of which has characters that resemble historical persons and a plot that parallels historical events. Apart from the conjuration which suggests the Popish Plot and the character Vinditius who resembles Titus Oates, little in *Lucius Junius Brutus* can be considered specifically allegorical. Its relevance to politics is thematic: the celebration of constitutionalism and the denunciation of royal tyranny; and this is inherent in the choice of subject. Any English

[14] Arthur L. Cooke and Thomas B. Stroup, "The Political Implications in Lee's *Constantine the Great*," *Journal of English and Germanic Philology*, XLIX (1950), 506–515.

play about Lucius Junius Brutus had to be a Whig play. Because allegory was unnecessary to make the political point, the play could have a focus on the career of its historical protagonist; and thus it could be more than merely a party piece to be interpreted with the aid of a key. Both *The Duke of Guise* and *Constantine the Great* suffer from the cleverness of their sustained parallels with historical events. By contrast *Lucius Junius Brutus* retains its integrity as a tragedy, possessing a political theme merely as a complicating and enriching dimension.

However important for the play Livy's *Ab Urbe Condita* may have been, Lee drew on other accounts of Brutus, fictional as well as historical.[15] He apparently consulted *The Roman Antiquities* of Dionysius of Halicarnassus, as would appear from his use of distinctive words that seem to be translations from that author; and he certainly consulted Plutarch's life of Valerius Publicola. The sacrificial scene early in Act IV, in which the conspirators pledge themselves in human blood to the conjuration while Vinditius (Vindicius) looks on from hiding, derives in some detail from Plutarch—though Livy also includes an account of Vindicius' spying. (We may indeed wonder if the aptness of the episode to current talk about secret meetings of Jesuits might not have attracted Lee to the subject.) And as Lee implies in his dedicatory epistle, he read Machiavelli's comments on Livy's account of Brutus, presumably taking from Machiavelli the conception of Brutus' exemplary judgment on his sons as necessary to the firm establishment of the Roman constitution.[16]

Still, it was not to the historians or political theorists that he turned for his principal elaborations on Livy's story but to a writer of historical fiction, Madeleine de Scudéry, whose *Clelia* (to use the English title of the translation he probably read) includes a long, romanticized version of Brutus' life from his boyhood to the execution of his sons. Lee had frequently looked to the French romances, and particularly those of Madeleine de Scudéry, for his subjects; his plays provide impressive testimony to the impact on Restoration drama

[15] My discussion of the sources of *Lucius Junius Brutus* is heavily indebted to William Van Lennep's review of the subject (see note 3, above), pp. 452–523.

[16] Cf. Machiavelli, *Discorsi sopra la Prima Deca di Tito Livio*, in *Opere*, ed. Mario Bonfantini (Riccardo Ricciardi Editore, Milano and Napoli), pp. 134–137, 316–317 (Book I, Chap. xvi; Book III, Chap. iii).

made by French romances. In several plays he used episodes from the lives of famous people of antiquity—Alexander the Great, Hannibal, Augustus Caesar, among others—and characteristically he used the French romances as supplements to the ancient historians, feeling no more reluctance than the French writers from whom he borrowed to depart from and elaborate on historical record. Thus in *Lucius Junius Brutus* he follows Madeleine de Scudéry in introducing a love affair to complicate a son's conflict of loyalties, though he departs from the French love plot in important particulars; and he does not follow Mlle. de Scudéry in depicting Brutus as once having been in love with Lucrece. Yet he may have expected his audience to know about the relationship as described in *Clelia*. The extended and detailed account of Brutus in the romance, which was widely read in London at the time Lee was writing, enabled him to assume a knowledge of events in Brutus' life not explained in the play: the reason, for example, why Brutus had assumed the disguise of stupidity (to protect himself from Tarquin, who had killed his brother and father and confiscated their property). In his frequently elliptical exposition, Lee wrote as though he was dramatizing well-known events, and so indeed he was except that many details are to be traced to Madeleine de Scudéry's historical fiction rather than to the classical historians. The major events and much of the moral and political interpretation of them are present in the historians; the emotional amplification derives in considerable measure from the French romance.

Livy and Madeleine de Scudéry are Lee's principal sources, and from both of them, as Professor Van Lennep demonstrated with precision, he borrowed specific detail. Yet if he followed their versions of the Brutus story, we may be sure that he also had in mind the great examples of Shakespeare's and Jonson's Roman plays *Julius Caesar* and *Catiline*, to both of which he refers in his dedication. One of the central set speeches of Lee's play, Brutus' oration over the body of Lucrece, contains in its opening line (II.i.139) an echo of the most famous speech in Shakespeare's play, Mark Antony's funeral oration for Caesar (III.ii.79 ff.). Perhaps too the prodigies that Titus sees (cf. IV.i.144 ff.) after he has pledged himself to the conspiracy derive from the prodigies that foreshadowed Shakespeare's Caesar's death (II, ii, 13 ff.). Lee's version of the conspiracy in favor of Tarquin sounds like accounts of Catiline's conspiracy, the dramatic version in Jonson's play as well as the versions in Cicero and Sallust. Lee may also have drawn suggestions from Otway's very different Roman play,

Brutus, the title character, whose legendary virtue provides the principal theme of the play; he dominates the action, and he is the center of interest. Yet it is Titus who has a tragic flaw—his uncontrollable love for Teraminta—that leads him to crime and finally to death; he rather than his father undergoes the tragic agony: sin, repentance, expiation. He would seem to be the good but imperfect man described by Aristotle as the most appropriate protagonist for tragedy. Brutus' exemplary nature precludes the human weaknesses that precipitate tragic events. Yet because he is the father of Titus he must suffer for Titus' faults, and in fact attention is focused in the catastrophe on Brutus rather than on his son, who becomes little more than the agent by which the father's devotion to duty can be demonstrated.

There are difficulties in the interpretation of the character of Titus. We are asked by implication to extend him our sympathy and to consider him as in a qualified sense admirable. Yet he shows remarkably little fortitude or perception. He violates a most solemn oath to his father in rejoining Teraminta after promising not to do so; and he promptly, it would appear half inadvertently, enters into a conspiratorial relationship with the deposed tyrant. These are grave crimes: understandable perhaps as the acts of an inexperienced and passionate youth, driven to the more serious crime of treason by fear for the safety of his wife, but still grave crimes. It was not unreasonable that the death penalty should have been imposed for the act of treason. The extenuating circumstances are less apparent to the reader than they seem to be to the Romans who plead with Brutus to spare his son. Brutus indeed shows fortitude in performing his duty and sentencing his son to death; but still—and this fact is obscured in Titus' self-congratulation and in the general amazement at Brutus' inflexibility—he was merely exacting a normal and expected punishment for high treason. The execution of Titus may represent an act of exemplary justice, but it is no judicial murder. In Livy the punishment is considered exemplary, severe but not unjust; and it is the exemplary (i.e., worthy of providing an example) nature of the punishment that Machiavelli emphasizes in his commentary on Livy. The sons of Brutus are guilty, and their father presides at their deserved execution. There is no ambiguity in Livy's implied evaluation of either son, and there is no sentimentality in the treatment of the episode. We find it difficult to respond as Lee demands to the plight of Titus; and we are intermittently repelled by the luxuriance of his passionate language. Lee lacked the discrimination to expunge occasional mawkish passages, with the result that some very bad lines remain.

Yet if the action involving Titus leads to emotional excess, it does not lead to a divergent line of action. Unlike the love plot in Addison's *Cato* (a play with important thematic similarities to *Lucius Junius Brutus*), this one is neither structurally nor thematically irrelevant. Titus' love for Teraminta provides an indispensable motive for the treasonous act that brings in its wake the exemplary punishment, the climactic event of the play. His divided allegiance, to his father and to his wife, parallels the divided allegiance of his father, to Rome and to his sons. The failure of Titus to make the right choice accentuates the nobility of his father's choice.

If structurally sound in this respect, the play has nevertheless been criticized for a breach in the unity of action. When Charles Gildon early in the eighteenth century prepared his adaptation of the play, he not only removed the passages that were dangerous politically and changed the locale to Renaissance Italy, but he also eliminated the scenes devoted to the rape of Lucrece, beginning his dramatic action after the expulsion of Tarquin.[18] He considered Lee's play to be faulty, as he explains in his preface, in its double focus: "First, the old play has plainly two distinct actions, one ending with the death of Lucretia, the other with the confirmation of the liberty of Rome by the death of the sons of Brutus and the other conspirators." The judgment is understandable, but it is one that would have more force to a neoclassical formalist critic than to a modern one. There are indeed two separate climactic events in the play, both famous events in early Roman history, but movement from the one to the other is rapid (though not rapid enough for the unity of time to be observed), and the later is causally related to the earlier. The rape of Lucrece leads to a revolt against Tarquin and the establishment of the Roman republic; a conspiracy against the republic is crushed and the conspirators punished in an act of justice which emphasizes the establishment of a rule of law. Lucrece and Brutus provide parallel examples of Roman inflexibility. If the dramatic action has a considerable complexity and magnitude, it is coherent enough, and it consistently serves the needs of the historical and political themes.

The emotional range of the play is broad, encompassing patriotism

[18] Voltaire's *Brutus*, which is independent of Lee's and Gildon's plays, also begins after the expulsion of Tarquin.

and family affection as well as sexual love; and the intellectual range, encompassing a theory of constitutional government, is even broader. Lee's themes hold a certain permanent interest, not limited by their relevance to the excitement created by the Popish Plot. We may understand more fully why Englishmen of his generation and the next liked to think of themselves as Augustans as we read this rendering of the moral and political ideals of Augustan Rome.

JOHN LOFTIS

Stanford University

. . . cæloque invectus aperto
Flectit equos curruque volans dat lora secundo.

Soon as the Sire, looking forth upon the
waters and driving under a clear sky,
guides his steeds and, flying onwards,
gives rein to his willing car.

Aeneid I.155–156

Trans. H. Rushton Fairclough (Loeb Library); erroneously identified
on the title page of the early editions as from the fourth rather than the first
book of the *Aeneid*.

To the Right Honorable Charles, Earl of Dorset and Middlesex, One of the Gentlemen of His Majesty's Bedchamber, etc.

My Lord,

With an assurance I hope becoming the justice of my
cause, I lay this tragedy at your lordship's feet, not as a
common persecution but as an offering suitable to your
virtue and worthy of the greatness of your name. There are 5
some subjects that require but half the strength of a great
poet, but when Greece or old Rome come in play, in nature,
wit, and vigor of foremost Shakespeare, the judgment and
force of Jonson, with all his borrowed mastery from the
ancients, will scarce suffice for so terrible a grapple. The 10
poet must elevate his fancy with the mightiest imagination,
he must run back so many hundred years, take a just
prospect of the spirit of those times without the least thought
of ours; for if his eye should swerve so low, his muse will
grow giddy with the vastness of the distance, fall at once, and 15
forever lose the majesty of the first design. He that will
pretend to be a critic of such a work must not have a grain
of Cecilius, he must be Longin throughout or nothing, where
even the nicest, best remarks must pass but for alloy to the
imperial fury of this old Roman gold. There must be no 20
dross through the whole mass, the furnace must be justly
heated, and the bullion stamped with an unerring hand.
In such a writing there must be greatness of thought without
bombast, remoteness without monstrousness, virtue armed
with severity, not in iron bodies, solid wit without modern 25
affectation, smoothness without gloss, speaking out without
cracking the voice or straining the lungs. In short, my lord,
he that will write as he ought on so noble an occasion must

2. becoming] *Q1, C1–3*; become
Q2.

Earl of Dorset] Sixth Earl of Dorset and Earl of Middlesex (1638–1706),
minor poet and generous patron of major poets. He is remembered as a
friend and benefactor of Dryden.
    18. *Cecilius*] Caecilius Statius, a Gaul who in the second century B.C.
went to Rome and wrote comedies.
    18. *Longin*] Longinus, Greek philosopher of the third century A.D., to
whom is attributed a famous treatise on the sublime.

write like you. But I fear there are few that know how to copy after so great an original as your lordship, because   30
there is scarce one genius extant of your own size that can follow you *passibus aequis*, that has the felicity and mastery of the old poets or can half match the thoughtfulness of your soul. How far short I am cast of such inimitable excellence, I must with shame, my lord, confess I am but too, too   35
sensible. Nature, 'tis believed (if I am not flattered and do not flatter myself), has not been niggardly to me in the portion of a genius, though I have been so far from improving it that I am half afraid I have lost of the principal. It behooves me then for the future to look about me to see   40
whether I am a lag in the race, to look up to your lordship and strain upon the track of so fair a glory. I must acknowledge, however I have behaved myself in drawing, nothing ever presented itself to my fancy with that solid pleasure as Brutus did in sacrificing his sons. Before I read Machivel's   45
notes upon the place, I concluded it the greatest action that was ever seen throughout all ages on the greatest occasion. For my own endeavor, I thought I never painted any man so to the life before.

> *Vis & Tarquinios reges animamq; superbam*   50
> *Ultoris Bruti, fascesque videre receptos?*
> *Infelix utcunque ferent ea facta Minores!*

No doubt that divine poet imagined it might be too great for any people but his own; perhaps I have found it so, but Jonson's Catiline met no better fate, as his motto from   55
Horace tells us.

---

35. but] *Q1, C1–3*; *om. Q2.*
35. too] *Q1–2, C1*; *om. C2–3.*
49. before.] *Q2, C1*; before *Q1.*
52. utcunque] *Q2, C1–3*; uctunque *Q1.*
52. *Minores!*] *Q1*; Minores? *Q2, C1–3.*

---

32. *passibus aequis*] "with equal steps."

45–46. *Machivel's . . . place*] Machiavelli, *Discorsi sopra la Prima Deca di Tito Livio*, in *Opere*, ed. Mario Bonfantini (Riccardo Ricciardi Editore, Milano and Napoli), pp. 134–137, 316–317 (Book I, Chap. xvi; Book III, Chap. iii).

50–52. *Vis . . . Minores!*] *Aeneid* VI. 817–818, 822. Trans. H. Rushton Fairclough (Loeb Library): "Wilt thou see, too, the Tarquin kings, and the proud soul of avenging Brutus, and the fasces regained? . . . Unhappy he, howe'er posterity extol that deed."

LUCIUS JUNIUS BRUTUS

. . . His non plebecula gaudet etc.

Nay, Shakespeare's Brutus with much ado beat himself
into the heads of a blockish age, so knotty were the oaks he
had to deal with. For my own opinion, in spite of all the   60
obstacles my modesty could raise, I could not help inserting
a vaunt in the title page, *Cæloque*, etc.

And having gained the list that he designed,
Bold as the billows driving with the wind,
He loosed the muse that winged his free-born mind.   65

On this I armed and resolved not to be stirred with the
little exceptions of a sparkish generation that have an an-
tipathy to thought. But, alas, how frail are our best resolves
in our own concerns. I showed no passion outward, but
whether through an over-conceit of the work, or because   70
perhaps there was indeed some merit, the fire burnt inward,
and I was troubled for my dumb play, like a father for his
dead child. 'Tis enough that I have eased my heart by this
dedication to your lordship. I comfort myself too, whatever
our partial youth allege, your lordship will find something   75
in it worth your observation, which with my future diligence,
resolution to study, devotion to virtue, and your lordship's
service, may render me not altogether unworthy the
protection of your lordship.

My lord,   80
Your lordship's most humble
and devoted servant,

NAT. LEE

68. thought.] thought: *Q2, C1–3*;   *C1–3*.
thought, *Q1*.   76. in it] *Q2, C1–3*; in in *Q1*.
69. concerns.] *Q1*; concerns? *Q2*,

57. *His . . . gaudet*] Horace, Epistles II.i. 186–188: *His nam plebecula gaudet.
verum equites quoque iam migravit ab aure voluptas omnis ad incertos oculos et gaudia
vana.* Trans. H. Rushton Fairclough (Loeb Library): " 'Tis in such things
the rabble delights. But nowadays all the pleasure even of the knights has
passed from the ear to the vain delights of the wandering eye."
62–65. *Cæloque . . . free-born mind.*] The English verses here, presumably
written by Lee himself, are not a translation of the Latin passage cited
(*Aeneid* I. 155–156) but are similar to them in meaning.

PROLOGUE TO BRUTUS
Written by Mr. Duke

Long has the tribe of poets on the stage
Groaned under persecuting critics' rage,
But with the sound of railing and of rhyme,
Like bees united by the tinkling chime,
The little stinging insects swarm the more,   5
And buzz is greater than it was before.
But O! You leading voters of the pit,
That infect others with your too much wit,
That well-affected members do seduce,
And with your malice poison half the house,   10
Know your ill-managed, arbitrary sway
Shall be no more endured but ends this day.
Rulers of abler conduct we will choose,
And more indulgent to a trembling muse;
Women for ends of government more fit,⎫   15
Women shall rule the boxes and the pit, ⎬
Give laws to love and influence to wit. ⎭
Find me one man of sense in all your roll,
Whom some one woman has not made a fool.
Even business, that intolerable load   20
Under which man does groan and yet is proud,
Much better they can manage would they please;
'Tis not their want of wit but love of ease.
For, spite of art, more wit in them appears,
Though we boast ours and they dissemble theirs.   25
Wit once was ours and shot up for a while
Set shallow in a hot and barren soil;
But when transplanted to a richer ground
Has in their Eden its perfection found.
And 'tis but just they should our wit invade,   30
Whilst we set up their painting, patching trade;
As for our courage, to our shame 'tis known,
As they can raise it, they can pull it down.

17. wit.] *Q2, C1–3*; wit, *Q1*.

Mr. Duke] Richard Duke (1659?–1711), like Lee a graduate of Trinity
College, Cambridge, was a poet and clergyman.

At their own weapons they our bullies awe,
Faith, let them make an antisalic law,   35
Prescribe to all mankind, as well as plays,
And wear the breeches as they wear the bays.

35. law,] *Q2, C1–3*; law *Q1.*

---

35. *antisalic law*] The salic law excluded females from succession to a throne. Hence, an antisalic law would restore rights to them.

DRAMATIS PERSONAE

Lucius Junius Brutus	*Mr. Betterton*
Titus	*Mr. Smith*
Tiberius	*Mr. Williams*
Collatinus	*Mr. Wiltshire*
Valerius	*Mr. Gillow*
Horatius	*Mr. Norris*
Aquilius	
Vitellius	
Junius	
Fecialian Priests	*Mr. Percival*
	Mr. Freeman
Vinditius	*Mr. Nokes*
Fabritius	*Mr. Jeron*
Citizens, &c.	

Women

Sempronia	*Lady Slingsby*
Lucrece	*Mrs. Betterton*
Teraminta	*Mrs. Barry*

Scene: *Rome*

Lucrece] Lucretia *Q 1–2, C1–3.*

Additional characters not listed in the *Dramatis Personae. Men:* Flaminius, Lartius, Lucretius, Mutius, Herminius, Trebonius, Servillius, Minutius, Pomponius. *Women:* Aquilia, Vitellia.

-8-

Lucius Junius Brutus;
Father of His Country

ACT I

[Enter] Titus, Teraminta.

TITUS.

O Teraminta, why this face of tears?
Since first I saw thee, till this happy day,
Thus hast thou passed thy melancholy hours,
Even in the court retired, stretched on a bed
In some dark room, with all the curtains drawn;   5
Or in some garden o'er a flow'ry bank
Melting thy sorrows in the murmuring stream;
Or in some pathless wilderness a-musing,
Plucking the mossy bark of some old tree;
Or poring, like a sibyl, on the leaves.   10
What, now the priest should join us! O, the gods!
What can you proffer me in vast exchange
For this ensuing night? Not all the days
Of crowning kings, of conquering generals,
Not all the expectation of hereafter,   15
With what bright fame can give in th'other world
Should purchase thee this night one minute from me.

TERAMINTA.

O, Titus! If since first I saw the light,
Since I began to think on my misfortunes,
And take a prospect of my certain woes,   20
If my sad soul has entertained a hope
Of pleasure here, or harbored any joy,
But what the presence of my Titus gave me;
Add, add, you cruel gods, to what I bear,

---

10. *sibyl*] in classical legend, a prophetess.

And break my heart before him.   25

TITUS.

Break first th'eternal chain, for when thou'rt gone
The world to me is chaos. Yes, Teraminta,
So close the everlasting sisters wove us,
Whene'er we part the strings of both must crack:
Once more I do entreat thee give the grave   30
Thy sadness. Let me press thee in my arms,
My fairest bride, my only lightness here,
Tune of my heart, and charmer of my eyes.
Nay, thou shalt learn the ecstasy from me,
I'll make thee smile with my extravagant passion,   35
Drive thy pale fears away, and e're the morn
I swear, O Teraminta, O my love,
Cold as thou art, I'll warm thee into blushes.

TERAMINTA.

O, Titus! May I, ought I to believe you?
Remember, sir, I am the blood of Tarquin;   40
The basest too.

TITUS.   Thou art the blood of heav'n,
The kindest influence of the teeming stars;
No seed of Tarquin. No, 'tis forged t'abuse thee.
A god thy father was, a goddess was his wife;
The wood nymphs found thee on a bed of roses,   45
Lapped in the sweets and beauties of the spring,
Diana fostered thee with nectar dews,
Thus tender, blooming, chaste, she gave thee me
To build a temple sacred to her name,
Which I will do, and wed thee there again.   50

TERAMINTA.

Swear then, my Titus, swear you'll ne'er upbraid me,
Swear that your love shall last like mine forever;
No turn of state or empire, no misfortune,
Shall e'er estrange you from me. Swear, I say,
That, if you should prove false, I may at least   55
Have something still to answer to my fate.

29. strings] *Q1, C1–3*; stings *Q2*.   36. thy] *Q1, C1–3*; my *Q2*.
35. my] *Q1, C1–3*; *om. Q2*.

28. *everlasting sisters*] the three Fates, who were considered to be weavers.

> Swear, swear, my lord, that you will never hate me,
> But to your death still cherish in your bosom
> The poor, the fond, the wretched Teraminta.

TITUS.

> Till death! nay, after death if possible.   60
> Dissolve me still with questions of this nature,
> While I return my answer all in oaths.
> More than thou canst demand I swear to do.
> This night, this night shall tell thee how I love thee.
> When words are at a loss, and the mute soul   65
> Pours out herself in sighs and gasping joys,
> Life grasps the pangs of bliss, and murmuring pleasures.
> Thou shalt confess all language then is vile,
> And yet believe me most without my vowing.

Enter Brutus with a Flamen.

> But see, my father with a flamen here!   70
> The court comes on; let's slip the busy crowd,
> And steal into the eternal knot of love.   *Exeunt.*

BRUTUS.

> Did Sextus, say'st thou, lie at Collatia,
> At Collatine's house last night?

FLAMEN.   My lord, he did.

> Where he, with Collatine and many others,   75
> Had been some nights before.

BRUTUS.   Ha! If before,

> Why did he come again?

FLAMEN.   Because, as rumor spreads,

> He fell most passionately in love with her.

BRUTUS.

> What then?

FLAMEN.   Why, is't not strange?

BRUTUS.   Is she not handsome?

FLAMEN.

> O, very handsome.

BRUTUS.   Then 'tis not strange at all.   80

> What, for a king's son to love another man's wife!

---

67. grasps] *C2–3*; grasps, *Q1–2, C1.*

69.1. *Flamen*] priest.
73. *Collatia*] a Sabine town near the Anio River.

Why, sir, I've known the king has done the same.
Faith, I myself, who am not used to caper,
Have sometimes had th'unlawful itch upon me.
Nay, prithee priest, come thou and help the number.   85
Ha! My old boy, the company is not scandalous.
Let's go to hell together. Confess the truth.
Didst thou ne'er steal from the gods an hour or so
To mumble a new prayer—
With a young fleshy whore in a bawdy corner? Ha!   90

FLAMEN.

My lord, your servant. —[*Aside.*] Is this the fool, the madman?
Let him be what he will, he spoke the truth.
If other fools be thus, they're dangerous fellows.   *Exit.*

BRUTUS (*solus*).

Occasion seems in view; something there is
In Tarquin's last abode at Collatine's.   95
Late entertained, and early gone this morning?
The matron ruffled, wet, and dropping tears,
As if she had lost her wealth in some black storm!
As in the body, on some great surprise,
The heart still calls from the discolored face,   100
From every part the life and spirits down,
So Lucrece comes to Rome and summons all her blood.
Lucrece is fair, but chaste as the fanned snow
Twice bolted o'er by the bleak northern blasts.
So lies this starry cold and frozen beauty,   105
Still watched and guarded by her waking virtue,
A pattern, though I fear inimitable,
For all succeeding wives. O Brutus! Brutus!
When will the tedious gods permit thy soul
To walk abroad in her own majesty,   110
And throw this visor of thy madness from thee?
O, what but infinite spirit, propped by fate,
For empire's weight to turn on, could endure
As thou hast done the labors of an age,
All follies, scoffs, reproaches, pities, scorns,   115
Indignities almost to blows sustained,

90. fleshy] *Q1*; fleshly *Q2, C1–3*.   104. bleak] *Q1, C1–3*; black *Q2*.
99. on] *Q1, C1–3*; or *Q2*.   109. thy] *Q1, C1–3*; my *Q2*.

For twenty pressing years, and by a Roman?
To act deformity in thousand shapes,
To please the greater monster of the two,
That cries, "Bring forth the beast, and let him tumble."   120
With all variety of aping madness,
To bray, and bear more than the ass's burden;
Sometimes to hoot and scream, like midnight owls,
Then screw my limbs like a distorted satyr,
The world's grimace, th'eternal laughingstock   125
Of town and court, the block, the jest of Rome.
Yet all the while not to my dearest friend,
To my own children, nor my bosom wife,
Disclose the weighty secret of my soul.
O Rome, O mother, be thou th'impartial judge   130
If this be virtue, which yet wants a name,
Which never any age could parallel,
And worthy of the foremost of thy sons.

Enter Horatius, Mutius.

MUTIUS.

Horatius, heard'st thou where Sextus was last night?

HORATIUS.

Yes, at Collatia. 'Tis the buzz of Rome.   135
'Tis more than guessed that there has been foul play,
Else, why should Lucrece come in this sad manner
To old Lucretius' house, and summon thither
Her father, husband, each distinct relation?

Enter Fabritius, *with courtiers.*

MUTIUS.

Scatter it through the city, raise the people,   140
And find Valerius out. Away, Horatius.
                    [Mutius *and* Horatius] *exeunt severally.*

FABRITIUS.

Prithee, let's talk no more on't. Look, here's lord Brutus.
Come, come, we'll divert ourselves. For 'tis but just that we
who sit at the helm should now and then unruffle our state

131. name,] *C2, C3*; name. *Q1–2,*   141. Away] *Q1, C1–3*; Way *Q2.
C1.*

–13–

affairs with the impertinence of a fool. Prithee, Brutus, 145
what's a clock?

BRUTUS.

Clotho, Lachesis, Atropos; the Fates are three. Let them but
strike, and I'll lead you a dance, my masters.

FABRITIUS.

But hark you, Brutus, dost thou hear the news of Lucrece?

BRUTUS.

Yes, yes; and I heard of the wager that was laid among you, 150
among you whoring lords at the siege of Ardea. Ha, boy!
About your handsome wives.

FABRITIUS.

Well; and how, and how?

BRUTUS.

How you bounced from the board, took horse, and rode like
madmen to find the gentle Lucrece at Collatia. But how 155
found her? Why, working with her maids at midnight. Was
not this monstrous and quite out of the fashion? Fine stuff
indeed, for a lady of honor, when her husband was out of
the way, to sit weaving, and pinking, and pricking of arras?
Now, by this light, my lord, your wife made better use of 160
her pincushion.

FABRITIUS.

My wife, my lord? By Mars, my wife!

BRUTUS.

Why should she not, when all the royal nurses do the same?
What, what, my lord, did you not find 'em at it, when you
came from Collatia to Rome? Lartius, your wife, and yours, 165
Flaminius, with Tullia's boys, turning the crystals up,
dashing the windows, and the fates defying? Now, by the
gods, I think 'twas civil in you, discreetly done, sirs, not to
interrupt 'em. But for your wife, Fabritius, I'll be sworn for
her, she would not keep 'em company.   170

158–159. for . . . way] *Q1, C1–3*;
om. Q2.

---

147. *Clotho . . . Atropos*] the names of the three Fates.

151. *Ardea*] town in Latium, conquered by the Romans in 442 B.C.

159. *arras*] tapestry.

166. *Tullia's boys*] Tullia, the wife of Tarquin, had three sons: Sextus,
Titus, and Arruns.

166. *crystals*] wine glasses.

FABRITIUS.

No marry would she not; she hates debauches. How have
I heard her rail at Terentia and tell her next her heart upon
the qualms that drinking wine so late and tippling spirits
would be the death of her?

BRUTUS.

Hark you, gentlemen, if you would but be secret now, I 175
could unfold such a business. My life on't, a very plot upon
the court.

FABRITIUS.

Out with it. We swear secrecy.

BRUTUS.

Why thus then. Tomorrow Tullia goes to the camp, and I
being master of the household have command to sweep the 180
court of all its furniture and send it packing to the wars.
Panders, sycophants, upstart rogues; fine knaves and surly
rascals; flatterers, easy, supple, cringing, passing, smiling
villains. All, all to the wars.

FABRITIUS.

By Mars, I do not like this plot.   185

BRUTUS.

Why, is it not a plot, a plot upon yourselves, your persons,
families, and your relations; even to your wives, mothers,
sisters, all your kindred? For whores too are included,
setters too, and whore-procurers; bag and baggage; all, all
to the wars. All hence, all rubbish, lumber out; and not a 190
bawd be left behind to put you in hope of hatching whores
hereafter.

FABRITIUS.

Hark, Lartius, he'll run from fooling to direct madness and
beat our brains out. The devil take the hindmost. Your
servant, sweet Brutus; noble, honorable Brutus.   195

[Fabritius *and courtiers*] *exeunt.*

Enter Titus.

TITUS.

'Tis done, 'tis done, auspicious heav'n has joined us,

188. kindred?]   *C1–3*;   kindred: 191. hope] *Q1, C1–3*; hopes *Q2*.
Q1–2.

189. *setters*] partners of swindlers.

    And I this night shall hold her in my arms.

    O, sir!

BRUTUS.   O, sir! That exclamation was too high.

    Such raptures ill become the troubled times;

    No more of 'em. And by the way, my Titus,   200

    Renounce your Teraminta.

TITUS.   Ha, my lord!

BRUTUS.

    How now, my boy?

TITUS.   Your counsel comes too late, sir.

BRUTUS.

    Your reply, sir,

    Comes too ill mannered, pert, and saucy, sir.

TITUS.

    Sir, I am married.

BRUTUS.   What, without my knowledge?   205

TITUS.

    My lord, I ask your pardon; but that Hymen—

BRUTUS.

    Thou liest. That honorable god would scorn it.

    Some bawdy flamen shuffled you together;

    Priapus locked you, while the bachanals

    Sung your detested epithalamium.   210

    Which of thy blood were the cursed witnesses?

    Who would be there at such polluted rites

    But goats, baboons, some chatt'ring old silenus

    Or satyrs grinning at your slimy joys?

TITUS.

    O, all the gods! My lord, your son is married   215

    To Tarquin's—

BRUTUS.   Bastard.

TITUS.   No, his daughter.

BRUTUS.   No matter.

    To any of his blood; if it be his,

    There is such natural contagion in it,

---

206. *Hymen*] god of marriage.

209. *Priapus*] god of fertility, considered to be lascivious.

209. *bachanals*] votaries of Bacchus.

213. *silenus*] a satyr.

Such a congenial devil in his spirit,
Name, lineage, stock, that but to own a part   220
Of his relation is to profess thyself
Sworn slave of hell and bondman to the furies.
Thou art not married.

TITUS.   O, is this possible?
This change that I behold? No part of him
The same; nor eyes, nor mien, nor voice, nor gesture!   225

BRUTUS.

O, that the gods would give my arm the vigor
To shake this soft, effeminate, lazy soul
Forth from thy bosom. No, degenerate boy,
Brutus is not the same; the gods have waked him
From dead stupidity to be a scourge,   230
A living torment to thy disobedience.
Look on my face, view my eyes flame, and tell me
If aught thou seest but glory and revenge,
A blood-shot anger, and a burst of fury,
When I but think of Tarquin. Damn the monster;   235
Fetch him, you judges of th'eternal deep,
Arraign him, chain him, plunge him in double fires.
If after this thou seest a tenderness,
A woman's tear come o'er my resolution,
Think, Titus; think, my son, 'tis nature's fault,   240
Not Roman Brutus but a father now.

TITUS.

O, let me fall low as the earth permits me,
And thank the gods for this most happy change,
That you are now, although to my confusion,
That awful, godlike, and commanding Brutus   245
Which I so oft have wished you, which sometimes
I thought imperfectly you were, or might be,
When I have taken unawares your soul
At a broad glance and forced her to retire.
Ah, my dear lord, you need not add new threats,   250
New marks of anger to complete my ruin,
Your Titus has enough to break his heart
When he remembers that you durst not trust him.
Yes, yes, my lord, I have a thousand frailties;
The mold you cast me in, the breath, the blood,   255

And spirit which you gave me are unlike
The godlike author; yet you gave 'em, sir.
And sure, if you had pleased to honor me,
T'immortalize my name to after ages
By imparting your high cares, I should have found   260
At least so much hereditary virtue
As not to have divulged them.

BRUTUS.   Rise, my son;
Be satisfied thou art the first that know'st me.
A thousand accidents and fated causes
Rush against every bulwark I can raise,   265
And half unhinge my soul. For now's the time
To shake the building of the tyrant down.
As from night's womb the glorious day breaks forth,
And seems to kindle from the setting stars,
So from the blackness of young Tarquin's crime   270
And furnace of his lust, the virtuous soul
Of Junius Brutus catches bright occasion.
I see the pillars of his kingdom totter.
The rape of Lucrece is the midnight lantern
That lights my genius down to the foundation.   275
Leave me to work, my Titus, O my son;
For from this spark a lightning shall arise
That must ere night purge all the Roman air,
And then the thunder of his ruin follows.
No more; but haste thee to Lucretius.   280
I hear the multitude and must among them.
Away, my son.

TITUS.   Bound and obedient ever.   *Exit.*

Enter Vinditius *with* plebeians.

FIRST CITIZEN.

Jupiter defend us! I think the firmament is all on a light fire.
Now, neighbor, as you were saying, as to the cause of
lightning and thunder, and for the nature of prodigies.   285

VINDITIUS.

What! A tailor, and talk of lightning and thunder? Why,
thou walking shred, thou moving bottom, thou upright

268. forth,] *Q2, C1–3*; forth. *Q1.*

---

needle, thou shaving edging skirt, thou flip-flap of a man,
thou vaulting flea, thou nit, thou nothing, dost thou talk of
prodigies when I am by? *O tempora! O mores!* But, neighbors, 290
as I was saying, what think you of Valerius?

ALL.

Valerius, Valerius!

VINDITIUS.

I know you are piping hot for sedition; you all gape for rebellion. But what's the near? For look you, sirs, we the people
in the body politic are but the guts of government; there- 295
fore, we may rumble and grumble and croak our hearts out
if we have never a head. Why, how shall we be nourished?
Therefore, I say, let us get us a head, a head, my masters.

BRUTUS.

Protect me, Jove, and guard me from the phantom!
Can this so horrid apparition be,   300
Or is it but the making of my fancy?

VINDITIUS.

Ha, Brutus! What, where is this apparition?

FIRST CITIZEN.

This is the tribune of the Celeres,
A notable headpiece, and the king's jester.

BRUTUS.

By Jove, a prodigy!   305

VINDITIUS.

Nay, like enough; the gods are very angry.
I know they are; they told me so themselves.
For look you, neighbors, I for my own part
Have seen today fourscore and nineteen prodigies and a half.

BRUTUS.

But this is a whole one. O, most horrible!   310
Look, Vinditius, yonder, o'er that part
O' the capitol, just, just there man, yonder, look.

VINDITIUS.

Ha, my lord!

---

289. *nit*] egg of a parasitic insect.
290. *O . . . mores!*] O what times! O what customs! (a Ciceronian
exclamation).
294. *near*] "nearer to one's end or purpose" (*OED*).
303. *tribune of the Celeres*] leader of the king's bodyguard.

BRUTUS.

    I always took thee for a quick-sighted fellow.
    What, art thou blind? Why, yonder, all o' fire,   315
    It vomits lightning. 'Tis a monstrous dragon.

VINDITIUS.

    O, I see it. O Jupiter and Juno! By the gods I see it.
    O neighbors, look, look, look on his filthy nostrils!
    'T has eyes like flaming saucers and a belly
    Like a burning caldron, with such a swinging tail!   320
    And O, a thing, a thing that's all o' fire!

BRUTUS.

    Ha! Now it fronts us with a head that's marked
    With Tarquin's name; and see, 'tis thunderstruck!
    Look yonder how it whizzes through the air!
    The gods have struck it down; 'tis gone, 'tis vanished.   325
    O neighbors, what, what should this portent mean?

VINDITIUS.

    Mean! Why, it's plain; did we not see the mark
    Upon the beast? Tarquin's the dragon, neighbors,
    Tarquin's the dragon, and the gods shall swinge him.

ALL.

    A dragon! A Tarquin!

FIRST CITIZEN.   For my part, I saw nothing.   330

VINDITIUS.

    How, rogue? Why, this is prodigy on prodigy!
    Down with him, knock him down. What, not see the dragon?

FIRST CITIZEN.

    Mercy, I did, I did; a huge monstrous dragon.

BRUTUS.

    So; not a word of this, my masters, not for your lives.
    Meet me anon at the Forum, but not a word.   335
    Vinditius, tell 'em the tribune of the Celeres
    Intends this night to give them an oration.

                                    Exeunt Vinditius *and* rabble.

317. O, I see] *Q1, C1–3*; O, see *Q2*.   Mercy: For my part *Q2*.
330. For my part] *Q1, C1–3*;   337.1. *Exeunt*] *Exit Q1–2*; *Ex. C1–3*.

    321. *thing*] male organ.
    329. *swinge*] whip.

Enter Lucrece, Valerius, Lucretius, Mutius, Herminius, Horatius,
Titus, Tiberius, Collatinus.

BRUTUS.

Ha! In the open air? So near, you gods?
So ripe your judgments? Nay, then let 'em break
And burst the hearts of those that have deserved them.   340

LUCRECE.

O Collatine! Art thou come?
Alas, my husband! O my love! My lord!

COLLATINUS.

O Lucrece! See, I have obeyed thy summons.
I have thee in my arms; but speak, my fair,
Say, is all well?

LUCRECE.   Away, and do not touch me.   345
Stand near, but touch me not. My father too!
Lucretius, art thou here?

LUCRETIUS.   Thou seest I am.
Haste, and relate thy lamentable story.

LUCRECE.

If there be gods, O, will they not revenge me?
Draw near, my lord, for sure you have a share   350
In these strange woes. Ah, sir, what have you done?
Why did you bring that monster of mankind
The other night to curse Collatia's walls?
Why did you blast me with that horrid visage,
And blot my honor with the blood of Tarquin?   355

COLLATINUS.

O all the gods!

LUCRECE.   Alas, they are far off,
Or sure they would have helped the wretched Lucrece.
Hear then, and tell it to the wond'ring world,
Last night the lustful, bloody Sextus came
Late and benighted to Collatia,   360
Intending, as he said, for Rome next morning;
But in the dead of night, just when soft sleep
Had sealed my eyes and quite becalmed my soul,

349. will they not] *Q 1–2*; will not
they *C1–3*.

—21—

Methought a horrid voice thus thundered in my ear,
"Lucrece, thou'rt mine, arise and meet my arms."   365
When straight I waked and found young Tarquin by me,
His robe unbuttoned, red and sparkling eyes,
The flushing blood that mounted in his face,
The trembling eagerness that quite devoured him,
With only one grim slave that held a taper,   370
At that dead stillness of the murd'ring night
Sufficiently declared his horrid purpose.

COLLATINUS.

O, Lucrece, O!

LUCRECE.

How is it possible to speak the passion,
The fright, the throes, and labor of my soul?   375
Ah, Collatine! Half dead I turned away
To hide my shame, my anger, and my blushes,
While he at first with a dissembled mildness
Attempted on my honor—
But hastily repulsed, and with disdain,   380
He drew his sword, and locking his left hand
Fast in my hair, he held it to my breast,
Protesting by the gods, the fiends, and furies,
If I refused him he would give me death,
And swear he found me with that swarthy slave   385
Whom he would leave there murdered by my side.

BRUTUS.

Villain! Damned villain!

LUCRECE.

Ah Collatine! O Father! Junius Brutus!
All that are kin to this dishonored blood,
How will you view me now? Ah, how forgive me?   390
Yet think not, Collatine, with my last tears,
With these last sighs, these dying groans, I beg you,
I do conjure my love, my lord, my husband,
O think me not consenting once in thought,
Though he in act possessed his furious pleasure.   395
For, O, the name, the name of an adulteress—

380. disdain,] *Q1*, *C1–3*; disdain
Q2.

But here I faint. O help me.
Imagine me, my lord, but what I was,
And what I shortly shall be, cold and dead.
COLLATINUS.
    O you avenging gods! Lucrece, my love,   400
    I swear I do not think thy soul consenting,
    And therefore I forgive thee.
LUCRECE.   Ah, my lord!
    Were I to live, how should I answer this?
    All that I ask you now is to revenge me;
    Revenge me, father; husband, O revenge me.   405
    Revenge me, Brutus; you his sons revenge me,
    Herminius, Mutius, thou Horatius too,
    And thou Valerius; all, revenge me all,
    Revenge the honor of the ravished Lucrece.
ALL.
    We will revenge thee.   410
LUCRECE.
    I thank you all; I thank you, noble Romans.
    And that my life, though well I know you wish it,
    May not hereafter ever give example
    To any that, like me, shall be dishonored,
    To live beneath so loathed an infamy,   415
    Thus I forever lose it, thus set free
    My soul, my life and honor all together.   *[Stabs herself.]*
    Revenge me; O revenge, revenge, revenge.   *Dies.*
LUCRETIUS.
    Struck to the heart, already motionless.
COLLATINUS.
    O give me way t'embalm her with my tears,   420
    For who has that propriety of sorrow,
    Who dares to claim an equal share with me?
BRUTUS.
    That, sir, dare I; and every Roman here.
    What now? At your laments, your puling sighs,
    And woman's drops? Shall these quit scores for blood,   425
    For chastity, for Rome, and violated honor?

417. S.D. *Stabs herself.*] S–C; *om.*
Q 1–2, C1–3.

Now, by the gods, my soul disdains your tears.
There's not a common harlot in the shambles
But for a drachma shall outweep you all.
Advance the body nearer. See, my lords,   430
Behold, you dazzled Romans, from the wound
Of this dead beauty thus I draw the dagger,
All stained and reeking with her sacred blood.
Thus to my lips I put the hallowed blade,
To yours Lucretius, Collatinus yours,   435
To yours Herminius, Mutius, and Horatius,
And yours, Valerius. Kiss the poniard round.
Now join your hands with mine, and swear, swear all,
By this chaste blood, chaste ere the royal villain
Mixed his foul spirits with the spotless mass,   440
Swear, and let all the gods be witnesses,
That you with me will drive proud Tarquin out,
His wife, th'imperial fury, and her sons,
With all the race; drive 'em with sword and fire
To the world's limits, profligate accurst.   445
Swear from this time never to suffer them,
Nor any other king, to reign in Rome.

ALL.

    We swear.

BRUTUS.

    Well have you sworn; and O, methinks I see
The hovering spirit of the ravished matron   450
Look down. She bows her airy head to bless you,
And crown th'auspicious sacrament with smiles.
Thus with her body high exposed to view
March to the Forum with this pomp of death.
O Lucrece! O!   455
When to the clouds thy pile of fame is raised
While Rome is free thy memory shall be praised.
Senate and people, wives and virgins all,

429. drachma] *Q1*; drachm *Q2,*
C1–3.
434. hallowed] *Q1, C2–3*; hollowed

Q2, C1.
441. all] *Q1, C1–3*; *om. Q2*.

428. *shambles*] brothel.

Shall once a year before thy statue fall;
Cursing the Tarquins, they thy fate shall mourn.   460
But when the thoughts of liberty return,
Shall bless the happy hour when thou wert born.   *Exeunt.*

ACT II

The Forum.

[*Enter*] Tiberius, Fabritius, Lartius, Flaminius.

TIBERIUS.

Fabritius, Lartius, and Flaminius,
As you are Romans, and obliged by Tarquin,
I dare confide in you. I say again,
Though I could not refuse the oath he gave us,
I disapprove my father's undertaking.   5
I'm loyal to the last, and so will stand.
I am in haste, and must to Tullia.

FABRITIUS.

Leave me, my lord, to deal with the multitude.

TIBERIUS.

Remember this in short. A king is one
To whom you may complain when you are wronged;   10
The throne lies open in your way for justice.
You may be angry, and may be forgiven.
There's room for favor, and for benefit,
Where friends and enemies may come together,
Have present hearing, present composition,   15
Without recourse to the litigious laws,
Laws that are cruel, deaf, inexorable,
That cast the vile and noble all together,
Where, if you should exceed the bounds of order,
There is no pardon. O, 'tis dangerous   20
To have all actions judged by rigorous law.
What, to depend on innocence alone,
Among so many accidents and errors
That wait on human life? Consider it;
Stand fast, be loyal. I must to the queen.   *Exit.* 25

FABRITIUS.

A pretty speech, by Mercury! Look you, Lartius, when the
words lie like a low wrestler, round, close and short, squat,
pat and pithy.

---

12. forgiven.] *Q1–2*; forgiven, *C1*;
forgiven; *C2–3.*

25. loyal.] loyal: *Q1*; loyal, *Q2,
C1–3.*

-26-

LARTIUS.

But what should we do here, Fabritius? The multitude will
tear us in pieces.   30

FABRITIUS.

'Tis true, Lartius, the multitude is a mad thing, a strange
blunder-headed monster, and very unruly. But eloquence is
such a thing, a fine, moving, florid, pathetical speech! But
see, the Hydra comes. Let me alone; fear not, I say, fear not.

Enter Vinditius *with* plebeians.

VINDITIUS.

Come, neighbors, rank yourselves, plant yourselves, set your-   35
selves in order. The gods are very angry, I'll say that for 'em.
Pough, pough, I begin to sweat already; and they'll find us
work enough today, I'll tell you that. And to say truth, I
never liked Tarquin before I saw the mark in his forehead.
For look you, sirs, I am a true commonwealth's man, and   40
do not naturally love kings, though they be good; for why
should any one man have more power than the people? Is
he bigger or wiser than the people? Has he more guts or
more brains than ·the people? What can he do for the
people that the people can't do for themselves? Can he make   45
corn grow in a famine? Can he give us rain in drought?
Or make our pots boil, though the devil piss in the fire?

FIRST CITIZEN.

For my part, I hate all courtiers, and I think I have reason
for't.

VINDITIUS.

Thou reason! Well, tailor, and what's thy reason?   50

FIRST CITIZEN.

Why, sir, there was a crew of 'em t'other night got drunk,
broke my windows, and handled my wife.

VINDITIUS.

How, neighbors? Nay, now the fellow has reason, look you.
His wife handled! Why, this is a matter of moment.

31. thing,] *C2–3*; thing; *Q1–2*;   36. order.] order; *Q1*; order, *Q2*,
thing? *C1*.   *C1–3*.

---

34. *Hydra*] many-headed monster.

FIRST CITIZEN.

>Nay, I know there were some of the princes, for I heard   55
>Sextus his name.

VINDITIUS.

>Aye, aye, the king's sons, my life for't; some of the king's
>sons. Well, these roaring lords never do any good among us
>citizens. They are ever breaking the peace, running in our
>debts, and swinging our wives.   60

FABRITIUS.

>How long at length, thou many-headed monster,
>You bulls and bears, you roaring beasts and bandogs,
>Porters and cobblers, tinkers, tailors, all
>You rascally sons of whores in a civil government,
>How long, I say, dare you abuse our patience?   65
>Does not the thought of rods and axes fright you?
>Does not our presence, ha, these eyes, these faces
>Strike you with trembling? Ha!

VINDITIUS.

>Why, what have we here? A very spitfire, the crack-fart of
>the court. Hold, let me see him nearer. Yes, neighbors, this 70
>is one of 'em, one of your roaring squires that poke us in the
>night, beat the watch, and deflower our wives. I know him,
>neighbors, for all his bouncing and his swearing. This is a
>court pimp, a bawd, one of Tarquin's bawds.

FABRITIUS.

>Peace, thou obstreperous rascal. I am a man of honor.   75
>One of the equestrian order; my name Fabritius.

VINDITIUS.

>Fabritius! Your servant, Fabritius. Down with him.
>Neighbors, an upstart rogue. This is he that was the queen's
>coachman and drove the chariot over her father's body.
>Down with him, down with 'em all. Bawds, pimps, panders. 80

FABRITIUS.

>O mercy, mercy, mercy!

VINDITIUS.

>Hold, neighbors, hold. As we are great, let us be just. You,

---

60. *swinging*] copulating with.
62. *bandogs*] dogs kept tied up.
66. *rods and axes*] fasces, symbol of authority of Roman magistrates.
79. *drove . . . body.*] Cf. Livy, *Ab Urbe Condita* I. xlviii. 6–7.

sirrah; you of the equestrian order, knight? Now, by Jove,
he has the look of a pimp. I find we can't save him. Rise,
sir knight, and tell me before the majesty of the people, what   85
have you to say that you should not have your neck broke
down the Tarpeian Rock, your body burnt, and your ashes
thrown in the Tiber?

FABRITIUS.

O! O! O!

VINDITIUS.

A courtier! A sheep biter! Leave off your blubbering and   90
confess.

FABRITIUS.

O! I will confess, I will confess.

VINDITIUS.

Answer me then. Was not you once the queen's coachman?

FABRITIUS.

I was, I was.

VINDITIUS.

Did you not drive her chariot over the body of her father,   95
the dead King Tullus?

FABRITIUS.

I did, I did, though it went against my conscience.

VINDITIUS.

So much the worse. Have you not since abused the good
people by seducing the citizens' wives to court for the king's
sons? Have you not by your bawd's tricks been the occasion 100
of their making assault on the bodies of many a virtuous
disposed gentlewoman?

FABRITIUS.

I have, I have.

VINDITIUS.

Have you not wickedly held the door while the daughters
of the wise citizens have had their vessels broken up?   105

FABRITIUS.

O, I confess, many a time and often.

VINDITIUS.

For all which services to your princes, and so highly
deserving of the commonwealth, you have received the
honor of knighthood?

---

90. *sheep biter*] thief or philanderer.

FABRITIUS.

    Mercy, mercy. I confess it all.   110

VINDITIUS.

    Hitherto I have helped you to spell. Now pray put together
    for yourself and confess the whole matter in three words.

FABRITIUS.

    I was at first the son of a carman, came to the honor of being
    Tullia's coachman, have been a pimp, and remain a knight
    at the mercy of the people.   115

VINDITIUS.

    Well, I am moved, my bowels are stirred. Take 'em away
    and let 'em only be hanged. Away with 'em, away with 'em.

FABRITIUS.

    O mercy! Help, help!

VINDITIUS.

    Hang 'em, rogues, pimps; hang 'em I say. Why, look you,
    neighbors, this is law, right, and justice; this is the people's 120
    law; and I think that's better than the arbitrary power of
    kings. Why, here was trial, condemnation, and execution,
    without more ado. Hark, hark; what have we here? Look,
    look, the tribune of the Celeres! Bring forth the pulpit, the
    pulpit.   *Trumpets sound a dead march.* 125

Enter Brutus, Valerius, Herminius, Mutius, Horatius, Lucretius,
Collatinus, Tiberius, Titus, *with the body of Lucrece.*

VALERIUS.

    I charge you fathers, nobles, Romans, friends,
    Magistrates, all you people, hear Valerius.
    This day, O Romans, is a day of wonders,
    The villainies of Tarquin are complete.
    To lay whose vices open to your view,   130
    To give you reasons for his banishment,
    With the expulsion of his wicked race,
    The gods have chosen Lucius Junius Brutus,
    The stupid, senseless, and illiterate Brutus,
    Their orator in this prodigious cause.   135
    Let him ascend, and silence be proclaimed.

VINDITIUS.

    A Brutus, a Brutus, a Brutus! Silence there.
    Silence, I say, silence on pain of death.

BRUTUS.

    Patricians, people, friends, and Romans all,
    Had not th'inspiring gods by wonder brought me   140
    From clouded sense to this full day of reason,
    Whence, with a prophet's prospect, I behold
    The state of Rome and danger of the world;
    Yet in a cause like this, methinks the weak,
    Enervate, stupid Brutus might suffice.   145
    O the eternal gods! Bring but the statues
    Of Romulus and Numa, plant 'em here
    On either hand of this cold Roman wife,
    Only to stand and point that public wound.
    O Romans, O, what use would be of tongues,   150
    What orator need speak while they were by?
    Would not the majesty of those dumb forms
    Inspire your souls and arm you for the cause?
    Would you not curse the author of the murder,
    And drive him from the earth with sword and fire?   155
    But where, methinks I hear the people shout,
    I hear the cry of Rome, where is the monster?
    Bring Tarquin forth, bring the destroyer out,
    By whose cursed offspring, lustful bloody Sextus,
    This perfect mold of Roman chastity,   160
    This star of spotless and immortal fame,
    This pattern for all wives, the Roman Lucrece
    Was foully brought to a disastrous end.

VINDITIUS.

    O, neighbors, O! I buried seven wives without crying,
    Nay, I never wept before in all my life.   165

BRUTUS.

    O the immortal gods, and thou great stayer
    Of falling Rome, if to his own relations
    (For Collatinus is a Tarquin too),
    If wrongs so great to them, to his own blood,
    What then to us, the nobles and the commons?   170
    Not to remember you of his past crimes,
    The black ambition of his furious queen,

---

147. *Romulus and Numa*] first and second kings of Rome.
166. *great stayer*] Jupiter (S-C).

Who drove her chariot through the Cyprian street
On such a damned design as might have turned
The steeds of day, and shocked the starting gods,   175
Blest as they are, with an uneasy moment.
Add yet to this, O, add the horrid slaughter
Of all the princes of the Roman senate,
Invading fundamental right and justice,
Breaking the ancient customs, statutes, laws,   180
With positive power and arbitrary lust;
And those affairs which were before dispatched
In public by the fathers, now are forced
To his own palace, there to be determined
As he and his portentous council please.   185
But then for you.

VINDITIUS.

Aye, for the people, come;
And then, my myrmidons, to pot with him.

BRUTUS.

I say, if thus the nobles have been wronged,
What tongue can speak the grievance of the people?   190

VINDITIUS.

Alas, poor people!

BRUTUS.

You that were once a free-born people, famed
In his forefathers' days for wars abroad,
The conquerors of the world; O, Rome! O, glory!
What are you now? What has the tyrant made you?   195
The slaves, the beasts, the asses of the earth,
The soldiers of the gods, mechanic laborers,
Drawers of water, taskers, timber-fellers,
Yoked you like bulls, his very jades for luggage,
Drove you with scourges down to dig in quarries,   200
To cleanse his sinks, the scavengers o' th' court;
While his lewd sons, though not on work so hard,
Employed your daughters and your wives at home.

VINDITIUS.

Yes, marry did they.

197. gods,] *C2–3*; gods *Q1–2, C1*.   court, *Q2*.
201. court;] *C1–3*;   court: *Q1*;

BRUTUS.

O all the gods! What are you Romans? ha! 205
If this be true, why have you been so backward?
O sluggish souls! O fall of former glory
That would not rouse unless a woman waked you!
Behold she comes and calls you to revenge her;
Her spirit hovers in the air and cries 210
"To arms, to arms; drive, drive the Tarquins out."
Behold this dagger taken from her wound,
She bids you fix this trophy on your standard,
This poniard which she stabbed into her heart,
And bear her body in your battle's front. 215
Or will you stay till Tarquin does return
To see your wives and children dragged about,
Your houses burnt, the temples all profaned,
The city filled with rapes, adulteries,
The Tiber choked with bodies, all the shores 220
And neighboring rocks besmeared with Roman blood?

VINDITIUS.

Away, away. Let's burn his palace first.

BRUTUS.

Hold, hold, my friends. As I have been th'inspirer
Of this most just revenge, so I entreat you,
O worthy Romans, take me with you still. 225
Drive Tullia out and all of Tarquin's race;
Expel 'em without damage to their persons,
Though not without reproach. Vinditius, you
I trust in this. So prosper us the gods,
Prosper our cause, prosper the commonwealth, 230
Guard and defend the liberty of Rome.

VINDITIUS.

Liberty, liberty, liberty!

ALL.

Liberty, etc. [Vinditius *and some others*] *exeunt.*

VALERIUS.

O Brutus, as a god we all survey thee;
Let then the gratitude we should express 235
Be lost in admiration. Well we know

236. Well] *Q1*; Well, *Q2, C1–3.*

Virtue like thine, so fierce, so like the gods,
That more than thou presents we could not bear,
Looks with disdain on ceremonious honors;
Therefore accept in short the thanks of Rome.   240
First with our bodies thus we worship thee,
Thou guardian genius of the commonwealth,
Thou father and redeemer of thy country.
Next we, as friends, with equal arms embrace thee,
That Brutus may remember, though his virtue   245
Soar to the gods, he is a Roman still.

BRUTUS.

And when I am not so, or once in thought
Conspire the bondage of my countrymen,
Strike me, you gods; tear me, O Romans, piecemeal,
And let your Brutus be more loathed than Tarquin.   250
But now to those affairs that want a view.
Imagine then the fame of what is done
Has reached to Ardea, whence the trembling king,
By guilt and nature quick and apprehensive,
With a bent brow comes post for his revenge   255
To make examples of the mutineers.
Let him come on. Lucretius, to your care
The charge and custody of Rome is given,
While we, with all the force that can be raised,
Waiting the Tarquins on the common road,   260
Resolve to join the army at the camp.
What thinks Valerius of the consequence?

VALERIUS.

As of a lucky hit. There is a number
Of malcontents that wish for such a time.
I think that only speed is necessary   265
To crown the whole event.

BRUTUS.   Go then yourself,
With these assistants, and make instant head
Well as you can, numbers will not be wanting,

255. revenge] *Q1*; revenge, *Q2*, *C1*.
C1–3.
260. Waiting] *C2–3*; Waving *Q1–2*, *C1–3*.
268. wanting,] *Q1*; wanting *Q2*,

242. *genius*] guardian spirit.

To Mars his field. I have but some few orders
To leave with Titus that must be dispersed,   270
And Brutus shall attend you.

VALERIUS.   The gods direct you.

Exeunt with the body of Lucrece. Manent Brutus, Titus.

BRUTUS.

Titus, my son?

TITUS.   My ever honored lord.

BRUTUS.

I think, my Titus,
Nay, by the gods, I dare protest it to thee,
I love thee more than any of my children.   275

TITUS.

How, sir, O how, my lord, have I deserved it?

BRUTUS.

Therefore I love thee more, because, my son,
Thou hast deserved it; for, to speak sincerely,
There's such a sweetness still in all thy manners,
An air so open, and a brow so clear,   280
A temper so removed from villainy,
With such a manly plainness in thy dealing,
That not to love thee, O my son, my Titus,
Were to be envious of so great a virtue.

TITUS.

O, all the gods, where will this kindness end?   285
Why do you thus, O my too gracious lord,
Dissolve at once the being that you gave me,
Unless you mean to screw me to performance
Beyond the reach of man?
Ah why, my lord, do you oblige me more   290
Than my humanity can e'er return?

BRUTUS.

Yes, Titus, thou conceiv'st thy father right,
I find our genii know each other well;
And minds, my son, of our uncommon make
When once the mark's in view never shoot wide,   295
But in a line come level to the white,
And hit the very heart of our design.
Then, to the shocking purpose. Once again
I say, I swear, I love thee, O my son;

   I like thy frame, the fingers of the gods   300
   I see have left their mastery upon thee,
   They have been tapering up thy Roman form,
   And the majestic prints at large appear.
   Yet something they have left for me to finish
   Which thus I press thee to, thus in my arms   305
   I fashion thee, I mold thee to my heart.
   What, dost thou kneel? Nay, stand up now a Roman,
   Shake from thy lids that dew that hangs upon 'em,
   And answer to th'austerity of my virtue.

TITUS.

   If I must die, you gods, I am prepared.   310
   Let then my fate suffice; but do not rack me
   With something more.

BRUTUS.   Titus, as I remember,
   You told me you were married.

TITUS.   My lord, I did.

BRUTUS.

   To Teraminta, Tarquin's natural daughter.

TITUS.

   Most true, my lord, to that poor virtuous maid,   315
   Your Titus, sir, your most unhappy son,
   Is joined forever.

BRUTUS.   No, Titus, not forever.
   Not but I know the virgin beautiful,
   For I did oft converse her when I seemed
   Not to converse at all. Yet more, my son,   320
   I think her chastely good, most sweetly framed,
   Without the smallest tincture of her father.
   Yet, Titus—Ha! What, man? What, all in tears?
   Art thou so soft that only saying "yet"
   Has dashed thee thus? Nay, then I'll plunge thee down, 325
   Down to the bottom of this foolish stream
   Whose brink thus makes thee tremble. No, my son,
   If thou art mine, thou art not Teraminta's;
   Or, if thou art, I swear thou must not be,
   Thou shalt not be hereafter.

TITUS.   O the gods!   330
   Forgive me, blood and duty, all respects
   Due to a father's name. Not Teraminta's!

BRUTUS.

No, by the gods I swear, not Teraminta's.
No, Titus, by th'eternal fates that hang
I hope auspicious o'er the head of Rome,   335
I'll grapple with thee on this spot of earth
About this theme till one of us fall dead.
I'll struggle with thee for this point of honor,
And tug with Teraminta for thy heart
As I have done for Rome. Yes, ere we part,   340
Fixed as you are by wedlock joined and fast,
I'll set you far asunder. Nay, on this,
This spotted blade, bathed in the blood of Lucrece,
I'll make thee swear on this thy wedding night
Thou wilt not touch thy wife.   345

TITUS.

Conscience, heart, and bowels,
Am I a man? Have I my flesh about me?

BRUTUS.

I know thou hast too much of flesh about thee.
'Tis that, my son, that and thy blood I fear
More than thy spirit, which is truly Roman.   350
But let the heated channels of thy veins
Boil o'er; I still am obstinate in this:
Thou shalt renounce thy father or thy love.
Either resolve to part with Teraminta,
To send her forth, with Tullia, to her father,   355
Or shake hands with me, part, and be accursed;
Make me believe thy mother played me false,
And, in my absence, stamped thee with a Tarquin.

TITUS.

Hold, sir, I do conjure you by the gods,
Wrong not my mother, though you doom me dead;   360
Curse me not till you hear what I resolve,
Give me a little time to rouse my spirits,
To muster all the tyrant-man about me,
All that is fierce, austere, and greatly cruel
To Titus and his Teraminta's ruin.   365

BRUTUS.

Remember me. Look on thy father's suff'rings,
What he has borne for twenty rolling years;

If thou hast nature, worth, or honor in thee,
The contemplation of my cruel labors
Will stir thee up to this new act of glory.   370
Thou want'st the image of thy father's wrongs;
O take it then, reflected with the warmth
Of all the tenderness that I can give thee.
Perhaps it stood in a wrong light before;
I'll try all ways to place it to advantage.   375
Learn by my rigorous Roman resolution
To stiffen thy unharassed infant virtue.
I do allow thee fond, young, soft, and gentle,
Trained by the charms of one that is most lovely;
Yet, Titus, this must all be lost when honor,   380
When Rome, the world, and the gods come to claim us.
Think then thou hear'st 'em cry, "Obey thy father."
If thou art false, or perjured, there he stands
Accountable to us; but swear t'obey;
Implicitly believe him that, if aught   385
Be sworn amiss, thou mayst have nought to answer.

TITUS.

What is it, sir, that you would have me swear,
That I may 'scape your curse and gain your blessing?

BRUTUS.

That thou this night will part with Teraminta.
For once again I swear if here she stays,   390
What for the hatred of the multitude
And my resolves to drive out Tarquin's race,
Her person is not safe.

TITUS.   Here, take me, sir;
Take me before I cool. I swear this night
That I will part with, O, my Teraminta.   395

BRUTUS.

Swear too, and by the soul of ravished Lucrece,
Though on thy bridal night, thou wilt not touch her.

TITUS.

I swear, even by the soul of her you named,

382. hear'st] *Q1*; heard'st *Q2*,
C1–3.

The ravished Lucrece—O th'immortal gods!
I will not touch her.
BRUTUS.   So. I trust thy virtue.   400
And, by the gods, I thank thee for the conquest.
Once more, with all the blessings I can give thee,
I take thee to my arms. Thus on my breast,
The hard and rugged pillow of thy honor,
I wean thee from thy love. Farewell; be fast   405
To what thou'st sworn, and I am thine forever.   *Exit.*
TITUS (*solus*).
To what thou'st sworn! O heaven and earth, what's that?
What have I sworn? To part with Teraminta,
To part with something dearer to my heart
Than my life's drops? What, not this night enjoy her?   410
Renounce my vows, the rights, the dues of marriage,
Which now I gave her, and the priest was witness,
Blessed with a flood that streamed from both our eyes,
And sealed with sighs, and smiles, and deathless kisses;
Yet after this to swear thou wilt not touch her!   415
O, all the gods, I did forswear myself
In swearing that, and will forswear again.
Not touch her! O thou perjured braggart; where,
Where are thy vaunts, thy protestations now?

Enter Teraminta.

She comes to strike thy staggering duty down.   420
'Tis fall'n, 'tis gone. O, Teraminta, come,
Come to my arms, thou only joy of Titus,
Hush to my cares, thou mass of hoarded sweets,
Selected hour of all life's happy moments;
What shall I say to thee?
TERAMINTA.   Say anything,   425
For while you speak methinks a sudden calm,
In spite of all the horror that surrounds me,
Falls upon every frighted faculty
And puts my soul in tune. O, Titus, O!
Methinks my spirit shivers in her house,   430
Shrugging, as if she longed to be at rest;
With this foresight, to die thus in your arms
Were to prevent a world of following ills.

TITUS.

    What ills, my love? What power has fortune now
    But we can brave? 'Tis true, my Teraminta,   435
    The body of the world is out of frame,
    The vast distorted limbs are on the rack
    And all the cable sinews stretched to bursting,
    The blood ferments, and the majestic spirit,
    Like Hercules in the envenomed shirt,   440
    Lies in a fever on the horrid pile.
    My father, like an Aesculapius
    Sent by the gods, comes boldly to the cure.
    But how, my love? By violent remedies,
    And says that Rome, ere yet she can be well,   445
    Must purge and cast, purge all th'infected humors
    Through the whole mass; and vastly, vastly bleed.

TERAMINTA.

    Ah, Titus! I myself but now beheld
    Th'expulsion of the queen, driven from her palace
    By the enraged and madding multitude,   450
    And hardly scaped myself to find you here.

TITUS.

    Why, yet, my Teraminta, we may smile.
    Come then to bed ere yet the night descends
    With her black wings to brood o'er all the world.
    Why, what care we? Let us enjoy those pleasures   455
    The gods have given; locked in each other's arms
    We'll lie forever thus, and laugh at fate.

TERAMINTA.

    No, no, my lord. There's more than you have named,
    There's something at your heart that I must find;
    I claim it with the privilege of a wife.   460
    Keep close your joys; but for your griefs, my Titus,
    I must not, will not lose my share in them.

434. S. P. TITUS.] *C1–3*; Ter. *Q 1–2*.   441. Lies] *Q 1–2*; Lie *C1–3*.
439. spirit] *Q 1–2*; spirits *C1–3*.

440–441.] The wife of Hercules gave him a garment which, having been
steeped in poison, tortured him when he put it on. He constructed a funeral
pile and had himself burned to death.
442. *Aesculapius*] god of medicine.

Ah, the good gods, what is it stirs you thus?
Speak, speak, my lord, or Teraminta dies.
O heav'ns, he weeps! Nay, then upon my knees   465
I thus conjure you speak, or give me death.

TITUS.

Rise, Teraminta. O, if I should speak
What I have rashly sworn against my love,
I fear that I should give thee death indeed.

TERAMINTA.

Against your love! No, that's impossible;   470
I know your godlike truth. Nay, should you swear,
Swear to me now that you forswore your love,
I would not credit it. No, no, my lord,
I see, I know, I read it in your eyes,
You love the wretched Teraminta still.   475
The very manner of your hiding it,
The tears you shed, your backwardness to speak
What you affirm you swore against your love
Tell me, my lord, you love me more than ever.

TITUS.

By all the gods, I do. O, Teraminta,   480
My heart's discerner, whither wilt thou drive me?
I'll tell thee then. My father wrought me up,
I know not how, to swear I know not what,
That I would send thee hence with Tullia,
Swear not to touch thee, though my wife; yet, O,   485
Hadst thou been by thyself, and but beheld him,
Thou wouldst have thought, such was his majesty,
That the gods light'ned from his awful eyes,
And thundered from his tongue.

TERAMINTA.   No more, my lord.
I do conjure you by all those powers   490
Which we invoked together at the altar,
And beg you by the love I know you bear me,
To let this passion trouble you no farther;
No, my dear lord, my honored godlike husband,
I am your wife, and one that seeks your honor.   495

477. speak] *Q2, C1–3*; speak, *Q1*.   487. thought,] *Q1, C1–3*; thought
481. whither] *C1–3*; whether *Q1–2*.   *Q2*.

By heaven, I would have sworn you thus myself.
What, on the shock of empire, on the turn
Of state, and universal change of things,
To lie at home and languish for a woman!
No, Titus, he that makes himself thus vile,   500
Let him not dare pretend to aught that's princely,
But be, as all the warlike world shall judge him,
The droll of th'people and the scorn of kings.

Enter Horatius.

HORATIUS.
My lord, your father gives you thus in charge,
Remember what you swore. The guard is ready;   505
And I am ordered to conduct your bride,
While you attend your father.

TITUS.   O, Teraminta!
Then we must part.

TERAMINTA.   We must, we must, my lord.
Therefore be swift, and snatch yourself away,
Or I shall die with ling'ring.

TITUS.   O, a kiss.   510
Balmy as cordials that recover souls,
Chaste as maids' sighs, and keen as longing mothers.
Preserve thyself; look well to that, my love.
Think on our covenant. When either dies,
The other is no more.

TERAMINTA.   I do remember,   515
But have no language left.

TITUS.   Yet we shall meet,
In spite of sighs we shall, at least in heaven.
O, Teraminta, once more to my heart,
Once to my lips, and ever to my soul.
Thus the soft mother, though her babe is dead,   520
Will have the darling on her bosom laid,
Will talk, and rave, and with the nurses strive,
And fond it still, as if it were alive;
Knows it must go, yet struggles with the crowd,
And shrieks to see 'em wrap it in the shroud.   525

512. mothers.] *Q1, C2–3*; mothers,
Q2, C1.

ACT III

[III.i]   [*Enter*] Collatinus, Tiberius, Vitellius, Aquilius.

COLLATINUS.
    Th'expulsion of the Tarquins now must stand;
    Their camp to be surprised while Tarquin here
    Was scolded from our walls! I blush to think
    That such a master in the art of war
    Should so forget himself.
VITELLIUS.   Triumphant Brutus,   5
    Like Jove when followed by a train of gods,
    To mingle with the fates and doom the world,
    Ascends the brazen steps o' the capitol,
    With all the humming senate at his heels;
    Even in that capitol which the king built   10
    With the expense of all the royal treasure,
    Ingrateful Brutus there in pomp appears,
    And sits the purple judge of Tarquin's downfall.
AQUILIUS.
    But why, my lord, why are not you there too?
    Were you not chosen consul by whole Rome?   15
    Why are you not saluted too like him?
    Where are your lictors, where your rods and axes?
    Or are you but the ape, the mimic god
    Of this new thunderer, who appropriates
    Those bolts of power which ought to be divided?   20
TIBERIUS.
    Now, by the gods, I hate his upstart pride,
    His rebel thoughts of the imperial race,
    His abject soul that stoops to court the vulgar,
    His scorn of princes, and his lust to the people.
    O, Collatine, have you not eyes to find him?   25
    Why are you raised but to set off his honors?
    A taper by the sun, whose sickly beams
    Are swallowed in the blaze of his full glory.

9. heels;] *Q1, C2–3*; heels, *Q2, C1.*   *C2–3.*
11. treasure,] *Q2, C1*; treasure: *Q1*,   24. people.] *C1–3*; people, *Q1–2.*

---

17. *lictors*] attendants of the chief magistrates who bore the fasces.

He, like a meteor, wades th'abyss of light,
While your faint luster adds but to the beard   30
That awes the world. When late through Rome he passed,
Fixed on his courser, marked you how he bowed
On this, on that side, to the gazing heads
That paved the streets and all embossed the windows,
That gaped with eagerness to speak, but could not,   35
So fast their spirits flowed to admiration,
And that to joy, which thus at last broke forth:
"Brutus, god Brutus, father of thy country!
Hail genius, hail! Deliverer of lost Rome!
Shield of the commonwealth and sword of justice!   40
Hail, scourge of tyrants, lash for lawless kings!
All hail," they cried, while the long peal of praises,
Tormented with a thousand echoing cries,
Ran like the volley of the gods along.

COLLATINUS.
No more on't; I grow sick with the remembrance.   45

TIBERIUS.
But when you followed, how did their bellying bodies,
That ventured from the casements more than half,
To look at Brutus, nay, that stuck like snails
Upon the walls, and from the houses' tops
Hung down like clust'ring bees upon each other;   50
How did they all draw back at sight of you
To laze, and loll, and yawn, and rest from rapture!
Are you a man? Have you the blood of kings
And suffer this?

COLLATINUS.
Ha! Is he not his father?

TIBERIUS.   I grant he is.   55
Consider this, and rouse yourself at home.
Commend my fire, and rail at your own slackness.
Yet more; remember but your last disgrace,
When you proposed, with reverence to the gods,
A king of sacrifices should be chosen,   60

47. half,] *Q1*; half *Q2, C1–3.*   57. your] *Q1, C1–3*; you *Q2.*

---

60. *king of sacrifices*] priest of high rank who performed certain rites
formerly devolving on the king.

And from the consuls. Did he not oppose you,
Fearing, as well he might, your sure election,
Saying it smelt too much of royalty,
And that it might rub up the memory
Of those that loved the tyrant? Nay, yet more,   65
That if the people chose you for the place,
The name of king would light upon a Tarquin,
Of one that's doubly royal, being descended
From two great princes that were kings of Rome?

COLLATINUS.

But after all this, whither wouldst thou drive?   70

TIBERIUS.

I would to justice, for the restoration
Of our most lawful prince. Yes, Collatine,
I look upon my father as a traitor;
I find that neither you, nor brave Aquilius,
Nor young Vitellius dare confide in me.   75
But that you may, and firmly, to the hazard
Of all the world holds precious, once again
I say, I look on Brutus as a traitor,
No more my father, by th'immortal gods.
And to redeem the time, to fix the king   80
On his imperial throne, some means proposed
That savor of a governed policy,
Where there is strength and life to hope a fortune,
Not to throw all upon one desperate chance,
I'll on as far as he that laughs at dying.   85

COLLATINUS.

Come to my arms. O thou so truly brave,
Thou may'st redeem the errors of thy race!
Aquilius and Vitellius, O embrace him,
And ask his pardon that so long we feared
To trust so rich a virtue. But behold,   90

Enter Brutus *and* Valerius.

Brutus appears. Young man, be satisfied,
I sound thy politic father to the bottom.

70. whither] *C1–3*; whether *Q1–2*.   86. brave,] *Q2, C1–3*; brave *Q1*.

Plotting the assumption of Valerius,
He means to cast me from the consulship.
But now I heard how he cajoled the people 95
With his known industry and my remissness,
That still in all our votes, proscriptions, edicts
Against the king, he found I acted faintly,
Still closing every sentence, "He's a Tarquin."

BRUTUS.

No, my Valerius, till thou art my mate, 100
Joint master in this great authority,
However calm the face of things appear,
Rome is not safe. By the majestic gods,
I swear, while Collatine sits at the helm,
A universal wrack is to be feared. 105
I have intelligence of his transactions.
He mingles with the young hot blood of Rome,
Gnaws himself inward, grudges my applause,
Promotes cabals with highest quality,
Such headlong youth as, spurning laws and manners, 110
Shared in the late debaucheries of Sextus,
And therefore wish the tyrant here again.
As the inverted seasons shock wise men,
And the most fixed philosophy must start
At sultry winters and at frosty summers, 115
So at this most unnatural stillness here,
This more than midnight silence through all Rome,
This deadness of discourse, and dreadful calm
Upon so great a change, I more admire
Than if a hundred politic heads were met 120
And nodded mutiny to one another,
More fear, than if a thousand lying libels
Were spread abroad, nay, dropped among the senate.

VALERIUS.

I have myself employed a busy slave,
His name Vinditius, given him wealth and freedom, 125

93. Valerius,] *Q1*; Valerius; *Q2*, *Q1*; consulship, *Q2*.
C1–3. 110. as,] *Q1*; as *Q2, C1–3*.
94. consulship.] *C1–3*; consulship: 113. shock] *Q1, C1–3*; shock'd *Q2*.

119. *admire*] wonder at.

To watch the motions of Vitellius
And those of the Aquilian family.
Vitellius has already entertained him,
And something thence important may be gathered,
For these of all the youth of quality   130
Are most inclined to Tarquin and his race
By blood and humor.
BRUTUS.   O, Valerius!
That boy, observ'st thou? O, I fear, my friend,
He is a weed, but rooted in my heart
And grafted to my stock. If he prove rank,   135
By Mars, no more but thus, away with him.
I'll tear him from me though the blood should follow.
Tiberius.
TIBERIUS.
My lord?
BRUTUS.   Sirrah, no more of that Vitellius;
I warned you too of young Aquilius.   140
Are my words wind that thus you let 'em pass?
Has thou forgot thy father?
TIBERIUS.   No, my lord.
BRUTUS.
Thou liest. But though thou scape a father's rod,
The consul's axe may reach thee. Think on that.
I know thy vanity and blind ambition.   145
Thou dost associate with my enemies.
When I refused the consul Collatine
To be the king of sacrifices, straight,
As if thou hadst been sworn his bosom fool,
He named thee for the office. And since that,   150
Since I refused thy madness that preferment,
Because I would have none of Brutus' blood
Pretend to be a king, thou hang'st thy head,
Contriv'st to give thy father new displeasure,
As if imperial toil were not enough   155
To break my heart without thy disobedience.
But by the majesty of Rome I swear,

135. stock.] stock; *Q1–2*; stock,   139. lord?] *Q1*; lord! *Q2, C1–3.*
C1–3.

If after double warning thou despise me,
By all the gods, I'll cast thee from my blood,
Doom thee to forks and whips as a barbarian,   160
And leave thee to the lashes of the lictor.
Tarquinius Collatinus, you are summoned
To meet the senate on the instant time.

COLLATINUS.

Lead on. My duty is to follow Brutus.
                    Exeunt Brutus, Valerius [,Collatinus].

TIBERIUS.

Now, by those gods with which he menaced me,   165
I here put off all nature. Since he turns me
Thus desperate to the world, I do renounce him;
And when we meet again he is my foe.
All blood, all reverence, fondness be forgot.
Like a grown savage on the common wild   170
That runs at all and cares not who begot him,
I'll meet my lion sire and roar defiance,
As if he ne'er had nursed me in his den.

Enter Vinditius *with the people and two* Fecialian priests *crowned with laurel, two spears in their hands, one bloody and half burnt.*

VINDITIUS.

Make way there, hey, news from the tyrant; here come
envoys, heralds, ambassadors. Whether in the gods' name   175
or in the devils' I know not, but here they come, your
Fecialian priests. Well, good people, I like not these priests.
Why, what the devil have they to do with state affairs?
What side soever they are for, they'll have heaven for their
part, I'll warrant you. They'll lug the gods in whether they   180
will or no.

FIRST PRIEST.

Hear, Jupiter, and thou, O Juno, hear;
Hear, O Quirinus; hear us all you gods

164.1. Collatinus] *S-C*; *om. Q 1–2, C1–3.*
C1–3.   183. gods] *Q 1*; gods, *Q 2, C1–3.*
176. devils'] divels *Q 1*; devils *Q 2,*

173.1. *Fecialian priests*] priests having special duties connected with declaring war and ratifying peace.
183. *Quirinus*] a war god, sometimes identified with Romulus or Mars.

Celestial, terrestrial, and infernal.

SECOND PRIEST.

Be thou, O Rome, our judge. Hear, all you people.   185

VINDITIUS.

Fine canting rogues! I told you how they'd be hooking the
gods in at first dash. Why, the gods are their tools and tackle;
they work with heaven and hell; and let me tell you, as
things go, your priests have a hopeful trade on't.

FIRST PRIEST.

I come ambassador to thee, O Rome,   190
Sacred and just, the legate of the king.

SECOND PRIEST.

If we demand, or purpose to require,
A stone from Rome that's contrary to justice,
May we be ever banished from our country,
And never hope to taste this vital air.   195

TIBERIUS.

Vinditius, lead the multitude away.
Aquilius, with Vitellius and myself,
Will straight conduct 'em to the capitol.

VINDITIUS.

I go, my lord, but have a care of 'em. Sly rogues I warrant
'em. Mark that first priest. Do you see how he leers? A   200
lying elder, the true cast of a holy juggler. Come, my
masters, I would think well of a priest but that he has a
commission to dissemble, a patent hypocrite that takes pay
to forge lies by law, and lives by the sins of the people.

Exeunt with people.

AQUILIUS.

My life upon't, you may speak out, and freely.   205
Tiberius is the heart of our design.

FIRST PRIEST.

The gods be praised. Thus then, the king commends
Your generous resolves, longs to be with you,
And those you have engaged, divides his heart
Amongst you, which more clearly will be seen   210
When you have read these packets. As we go,
I'll spread the bosom of the king before you.   *Exeunt.*

204. forge] *Q2, C1–3*; forge; *Q1.*

[III.ii]   *The Senate.*

BRUTUS.

   Patricians, that long stood and scaped the tyrant,
   The venerable molds of your forefathers,
   That represent the wisdom of the dead;
   And you the conscript chosen for the people,
   Engines of power, severest counselors,   5
   Courts that examine treasons to the head,
   All hail. The consul begs th'auspicious gods,
   And binds Quirinus by his tutelar vow,
   That plenty, peace, and lasting liberty
   May be your portion, and the lot of Rome.   10
   Laws, rules, and bounds, prescribed for raging kings,
   Like banks and bulwarks for the mother seas,
   Though 'tis impossible they should prevent
   A thousand daily wracks and nightly ruins,
   Yet help to break those rolling inundations   15
   Which else would overflow and drown the world.
   Tarquin, to feed whose fathomless ambition
   And ocean luxury, the noblest veins
   Of all true Romans were like rivers emptied,
   Is cut from Rome, and now he flows full on;   20
   Yet, fathers, ought we much to fear his ebb,
   And strictly watch the dams that we have raised.
   Why should I go about? The Roman people
   All, with one voice, accuse my fellow consul.

COLLATINUS.

   The people may; I hope the nobles will not.   25
   The people! Brutus does indulge the people.

BRUTUS.

   Consul, in what is right I will indulge 'em.
   And much I think 'tis better so to do,
   Than see 'em run in tumults through the streets,
   Forming cabals, plotting against the senate,   30
   Shutting their shops and flying from the town,

---

1 ff. *Brutus' speech*] Stroup and Cooke point out (S-C, II, 594) that Lee
follows the form of a classical oration.
23. *go about*] "use circumlocution" (*OED*).

As if the gods had sent the plague among 'em.
I know too well you and your royal tribe
Scorn the good people, scorn the late election,
Because we chose these fathers for the people   35
To fill the place of those whom Tarquin murdered.
And, though you laugh at this, you and your train,
The irreligious, harebrained youth of Rome,
The ignorant, the slothful, and the base;
Yet wise men know 'tis very rarely seen   40
That a free people should desire the hurt
Of common liberty. No, Collatine,
For those desires arise from their oppression,
Or from suspicion they are falling to it;
But put the case that those their fears were false,   45
Ways may be found to rectify their errors.
For grant the people ignorant of themselves,
Yet they are capable of being told,
And will conceive a truth from worthy men.
From you they will not, nor from your adherents,   50
Rome's infamous and execrable youth,
Foes to religion and the commonwealth,
To virtue, learning, and all sober arts
That bring renown and profit to mankind;
Such as had rather bleed beneath a tyrant,   55
To become dreadful to the populace,
To spread their lusts and dissoluteness round,
Though at the daily hazard of their lives,
Than live at peace in a free government,
Where every man is master of his own,   60
Sole lord at home, and monarch of his house,
Where rancor and ambition are extinguished,
Where universal peace extends her wings,
As if the golden age returned, where all
The people do agree and live secure,   65
The nobles and the princes loved and reverenced,

50. adherents,] *Q1*, *C1–3*; adherents. *Q2*.
53. arts] *Q1*, *C1–3*; arts, *Q2*.
59. government,] *Q1*, *C1–3*; government. *Q2*.
66. reverenced,] *Q1*, *C2–3*; reverenced; *Q2*; reverenced *C1*.

−51−

The world in triumph, and the gods adored.

COLLATINUS.

The consul, conscript fathers, says the people,
For divers reasons, grudge the dignity
Which I possessed by general approbation.   70
I hear their murmurs, and would know of Brutus
What they would have me do, what's their desire.

BRUTUS.

Take hence the royal name, resign thy office;
Go as a friend, and of thy own accord,
Lest thou be forced to what may seem thy will.   75
The city renders thee what is thy own
With vast increase, so thou resolve to go;
For till the name, the race, and family
Of Tarquin be removed, Rome is not free.

COLLATINUS.

Brutus, I yield my office to Valerius,   80
Hoping, when Rome has tried my faith by exile,
She will recall me. So the gods preserve you.   *Exit.*

BRUTUS.

Welcome Publicola, true son of Rome.
On such a pilot in the roughest storm
She may securely sleep and rest her cares.   85

    Enter Tiberius, Aquilius, Vitellius, *and the* Priests.

FIRST PRIEST.

Hear Jupiter, Quirinus, all you gods,
Thou father, judge commissioned for the message,
Pater Patratus for the embassy,
And sacred oaths which I must swear for truth,
Dost thou commission me to seal the peace,   90
If peace they choose; or hurl this bloody spear,
Half burnt in fire, if they enforce a war?

70. approbation.] approbation, *Q1–*   87. judge] *Q1*; judge, *Q2, C1–3.*
2; approbation: *C2–3*; approbation;   87. message,] *Q2, C1–3;* message
C1.   *Q1.*
71. and] *Q2, C1–3;* an *Q1.*

83. *Publicola*] honorary name bestowed on Valerius.
88. *Pater Patratus*] the leader of the Fecialian priests and thus of the
embassy negotiating for war or peace.
91–92. *hurl . . .fire*] ceremonial means of declaring war.

SECOND PRIEST.

    Speak to the senate and the Alban people
    The words of Tarquin. This is your commission.

FIRST PRIEST.

    The king, to show he has more moderation   95
    Than those that drove him from his lawful empire,
    Demands but restitution of his own,
    His royal household stuff, imperial treasure,
    His gold, his jewels, and his proper state
    To be transported where he now resides.   100
    I swear that this is all the king requires;
    Behold his signet set upon the wax.
    'Tis sealed and written in these sacred tables.
    To this I swear; and as my oath is just,
    Sincere, and punctual, without all deceit,   105
    May Jupiter and all the gods reward me.
    But if I act, or otherwise imagine,
    Think, or design, than what I here have sworn
    All you the Alban people being safe,
    Safe in your country, temples, sepulchers,   110
    Safe in your laws, and proper household gods;
    Let me alone be struck, fall, perish, die,
    As now this stone falls from my hand to earth.

BRUTUS.

    The things you ask, being very controversial,
    Require some time. Should we deny the tyrant   115
    What was his own, 'twould seem a strange injustice,
    Though he had never reigned in Rome; yet, fathers,
    If we consent to yield to his demand,
    We give him then full power to make a war.
    'Tis known to you, the Fecialian priests,   120
    No act of senate after sunset stands;
    Therefore, your offers being of great moment,
    We shall defer your business till the morn,
    With whose first dawn we summon all the fathers

111. gods;] *Q1*; gods, *C1–3*; goods,
Q2.

---

   93. *Alban people*] Romans, so called from the ancient town Alba Longa,
which had colonized Rome.

To give th'affair dispatch. So Jove protect,   125
Guard, and defend the commonwealth of Rome.   *Exeunt.*
                    Manent Tiberius, Aquilius, Vitellius, Priests.

TIBERIUS.

Now to the garden, where I'll bring my brother.
Fear not, my lord; we have the means to work him.
It cannot fail.

FIRST PRIEST.   And you, Vitellius, haste
With good Aquilius, spread the news through Rome,   130
To all of royal spirit; most to those
Young noblemen that used to range with Sextus.
Persuade a restitution of the king,
Give 'em the hint to let him in by night,
And join their forces with th'imperial troops,   135
For 'tis a shove, a push of fate, must bear it.
For you, the hearts and souls of enterprise,
I need not urge a reason after this.
What good can come of such a government
Where, though two consuls, wise and able persons   140
As are throughout the world, sit at the helm,
A very trifle cannot be resolved;
A trick, a start, a shadow of a business
That would receive dispatch in half a minute
Were the authority but rightly placed   145
In Rome's most lawful king? But now no more;
The Fecialian garden is the place
Where more of our sworn function will be ready
To help the royal plot. Disperse and prosper.

[III.iii]   *The Fecialian garden.*

TITUS (*solus*).

She's gone, and I shall never see her more,
Gone to the camp, to the harsh trade of war,
Driven from thy bed, just warm within thy breast,
Torn from her harbor by thy father's hand,

136. it.] it, *Q1*; it; *Q2, C1*; it:
C2–3.

0.1. *Fecialian garden*] presumably the enclosure on the Capitoline Hill
where the priests gathered sacred herbs.

Perhaps to starve upon the barren plain,   5
Thy virgin wife, the very blush of maids,
The softest bosom sweet, and not enjoyed.
O the immortal gods! And as she went,
Howe'er she seemed to bear our parting well,
Methought she mixed her melting with disdain,   10
A cast of anger through her shining tears,
So to abuse her hopes and blast her wishes
By making her my bride, but not a woman!

Enter Tiberius, Aquilius, Vitellius, *and* Priests, *with* Teraminta.

TIBERIUS.
　　See where he stands, drowned in his melancholy.
FIRST PRIEST.
　　Madam, you know the pleasure of the queen,   15
　　And what the royal Tullia did command
　　I've sworn to execute.
TERAMINTA.　　　　　　　　I am instructed.
　　Since then my life's at stake, you need not doubt
　　But I will act with all the force I can.
　　Let me entreat you leave me here alone   20
　　Some minutes, and I'll call you to the conquest.
　　　　　　　　　　　Exeunt Tiberius, Aquilius, Vitellius, Priests.
TITUS.
　　Choose then the gloomiest place through all the grove,
　　Throw thy abandoned body on the ground,
　　With thy bare breast lie wedded to the dew;
　　Then, as thou drink'st the tears that trickle from thee,   25
　　So stretched resolve to lie till death shall seize thee;
　　Thy sorrowful head hung o'er some tumbling stream
　　To rock thy griefs with melancholy sounds,
　　With broken murmurs and redoubled groans
　　To help the gurgling of the waters fall.   30
TERAMINTA (*aside*).
　　O, Titus, O, what scene of death is this!
TITUS.
　　Or if thy passion will not be kept in,

5. plain,] *Q1*; plain. *Q2, C1–3*.   7. bosom] *Q1*; bosom, *Q2, C1–3*.

As in that glass of nature thou shalt view
Thy swollen, drowned eyes with the inverted banks,
The tops of willows and their blossoms turned,   35
With all the under sky ten fathom down,
Wish that the shadow of the swimming globe
Were so indeed that thou might'st leap at fate,
And hurl thy fortune headlong at the stars.
Nay, do not bear it, turn thy wat'ry face   40
To yond misguided orb, and ask the gods
For what bold sin they doom the wretched Titus
To such a loss as that of Teraminta?
O Teraminta! I will groan thy name
Till the tired echo faint with repetition,   45
Till all the breathless grove and quiet myrtles
Shake with my sighs as if a tempest bowed 'em.
Nothing but Teraminta. O Teraminta!

TERAMINTA.

Nothing but Titus, Titus and Teraminta!
Thus let me rob the fountains and the groves,   50
Thus gird me to thee with the fastest knot
Of arms and spirits that would clasp thee through.
Cold as thou art, and wet with night's fall'n dews,
Yet dearer so, thus richly dressed with sorrows,
Than if the gods had hung thee round with kingdoms.   55
O, Titus, O!

TITUS.   I find thee Teraminta,
Waked from a fearful dream, and hold thee fast.
'Tis real, and I give thee back thy joys,
Thy boundless love with pleasures running o'er;
Nay, as thou art, thus with thy trappings, come,   60
Leap to my heart, and ride upon the pants,
Triumphing thus, and now defy our stars.
But, O, why do we lose this precious moment!
The bliss may yet be barred if we delay,
As 'twas before. Come to thy husband's bed.   65
I will not think this true till there I hold thee
Locked in my arms. Leave this contagious air;
There will be time for talk how thou cam'st hither

38. might'st] *Q2, C1–3*; migh'st *Q1*.

When we have been before hand with the gods.
Till then—

TERAMINTA.   O, Titus, you must hear me first.   70
I bring a message from the furious queen.
I promised, nay, she swore me not to touch you,
Till I had charmed you to the part of Tarquin.

TITUS.
Ha, Teraminta! Not to touch thy husband,
Unless he prove a villain?

TERAMINTA.   Titus, no.   75
I'm sworn to tell you that you are a traitor,
If you refuse to fight the royal cause.

TITUS.
Hold, Teraminta.

TERAMINTA.   No, my lord; 'tis plain,
And I am sworn to lay my reasons home.
Rouse then, awake, recall your sleeping virtue;   80
Side with the king, and arm against your father,
Take part with those that loyally have sworn
To let him in by night. Vitellius,
Aquilius, and your brother wait without;
Therefore I charge you haste, subscribe your name,   85
And send your vowed obedience to the king.
'Tis Teraminta that entreats you thus,
Charms, and conjures you. Tell the royal heralds
You'll head their enterprise. And then, my lord,
My love, my noble husband, I'll obey you,   90
And follow to your bed.

TITUS.   Never, I swear.
O, Teraminta, thou hast broke my heart.
By all the gods, from thee this was too much.
Farewell, and take this with thee. For thy sake,
I will not fight against the king, nor for him.   95
I'll fly my father, brother, friends forever,
Forsake the haunts of men; converse no more
With aught that's human; dwell with endless darkness.
For, since the sight of thee is now unwelcome,

72. promised,] *Q2, C1–3*; promised
Q1.

What has the world besides that I can bear?   100

TERAMINTA.

    Come back, my lord. By those immortal pow'rs
You now invoked, I'll fix you in this virtue.
Your Teraminta did but try how strong
Your honor stood; and now she finds it lasting,
Will die to root you in this solid glory.   105
Yes, Titus, though the queen has sworn to end me,
Though both the Fecialians have commission
To stab me in your presence if not wrought
To serve the king, yet by the gods I charge you
Keep to the point your constancy has gained.   110
Tarquin, although my father, is a tyrant,
A bloody black usurper; so I beg you
Even in my death to view him.

TITUS.   O you gods!

TERAMINTA.

    Yet guilty as he is, if you behold him
Hereafter with his wounds upon the earth,   115
Titus, for my sake, for poor Teraminta,
Who rather died than you should lose your honor,
Do not you strike him, do not dip your sword
In Tarquin's blood, because he was my father.

TITUS.

    No, Teraminta, no. By all the gods,   120
I will defend him, ev'n against my father.
See, see, my love; behold the flight I take.
What all the charms of thy expected bed
Could not once move my soul to think of acting,
Thy tears and menaced death, by which thou striv'st   125
To fix me to the principles of glory,
Have wrought me off. Yes, yes, you cruel gods,
Let the eternal bolts that bind this frame
Start from their order! Since you push me thus
Ev'n to the margin of this wide despair,   130
Behold I plunge at once in this dishonor,
Where there is neither shore nor hope of haven,
No floating mark through all the dismal vast.

132. haven] *Q 1–2*; heav'n *C1–3*.

'Tis rockless too, no cliff to clamber up
To gaze about and pause upon the ruin.   135
TERAMINTA.
    Is then your purposed honor come to this?
    What now, my lord?
TITUS.   Thy death, thy death, my love.
    I'll think on that and laugh at all the gods.
    Glory, blood, nature, ties of reverence,
    The dues of birth, respect of parents, all,   140
    All are as this, the air I drive before me.
    What ho! Vitellius and Aquilius, come,
    And you the Fecialian heralds, haste,
    I'm ready for the leap, I'll take it with you
    Though deep as to the fiends.   145
TERAMINTA.
    Thus hear me, Titus.
TITUS.   Off from my knees, away.
    What on this theme, thy death? Nay, stabbed before me!

        Enter Priests, *with* Tiberius, Aquilius, Vitellius.

    Speak not; I will not know thee on this subject,
    But push thee from my heart, with all persuasions
    That now are lost upon me. O, Tiberius,   150
    Aquilius, and Vitellius, welcome, welcome.
    I'll join you in the conjuration, come.
    I am as free as he that dares be foremost.
TERAMINTA.
    My lord, my husband.
TITUS.   Take this woman from me.
    Nay look you, sirs, I am not yet so gone,   155
    So headlong neither in this damned design
    To quench this horrid thirst with Brutus' blood.
    No, by th'eternal gods, I bar you that;
    My father shall not bleed.
TIBERIUS.   You could not think
    Your brother sure so monstrous in his kind,   160
    As not to make our father's life his care.

156. this] *Q 1–2*; his *C1–3*.

---

152. *conjuration*] conspiracy.

TITUS.

    Thus then, my lords, I list myself among you,
    And with my style in short subscribe myself
    The servant to the king. My words are these:
    "Titus to the king,   165
    Sir, you need only know my brother's mind
    To judge of me, who am resolved to serve you."

FIRST PRIEST.

    'Tis full enough.

TITUS.   Then leave me to the hire

          Exeunt Tiberius, Aquilius, Vitellius, *and* Priests.

    Of this hard labor, to the dear-bought prize,
    Whose life I purchased with my loss of honor.   170
    Come to my breasts, thou tempest-beaten flower,
    Brimful of rain, and stick upon my heart.
    O short-lived rose! Yet I some hours will wear thee.
    Yes, by the gods, I'll smell thee till I languish,
    Rifle thy sweets, and run thee o'er and o'er,   175
    Fall like the night upon thy folding beauties,
    And clasp thee dead. Then, like the morning sun,
    With a new heat kiss thee to life again,
    And make the pleasure equal to the pain.

165. king,] *Q1–2*; king: *C1–3*.

ACT IV

[*Enter*] Tiberius, Vitellius.

TIBERIUS.
    Hark, are we not pursued?
VITELLIUS.   No; 'tis the tread
    Of our own friends that follow in the dark.
TIBERIUS.
    What's now the time?
VITELLIUS.   Just dead of night,
    And 'tis the blackest that e'er masked a murder.
TIBERIUS.
    It likes me better, for I love the scowl,   5
    The grimmest lower of fate on such a deed.
    I would have all the charnel-houses yawn,
    The dusty urns and monumental bones
    Removed, to make our massacre a tomb.
    Hark! Who was that that holloed "Fire?"
VITELLIUS.   A slave   10
    That snores i 'th' hall, he bellows in his sleep
    And cries, "The capitol's o' fire."
TIBERIUS.   I would it were,
    And Tarquin at the gates. 'Twould be a blaze,
    A beacon fit to light a king of blood,
    That vows at once the slaughter of the world.   15
    Down with their temples, set 'em on a flame!
    What should they do with houses for the gods,
    Fat fools, the lazy magistrates of Rome,
    Wise citizens, the politic heads o' th' people,
    That preach rebellion to the multitude?   20
    Shy, let 'em off and roll into their graves.

[*Enter* Aquilius, Trebonius, Servilius, Minutius, Pomponius *with prisoners for sacrifice.*]

    I long to be at work. See, good Aquilius,
    Trebonius too, Servilius and Minutius,
    Pomponius hail. Nay, now you may unmask,
    Browbeat the fates and say they are your slaves.   25

16. flame!] flame? *Q1*; flame; *Q2*,
C1–3.

AQUILIUS.

What are those bodies for?

TIBERIUS.   A sacrifice.

These were two very busy commonwealth's men,
That, ere the king was banished by the senate,
First set the plot on foot in public meetings,
That would be holding forth 'twas possible   30
That kings themselves might err and were but men,
The people were not beasts for sacrifice;
Then jogged his brother, this crammed statesman here,
The bolder rogue, whom ev'n with open mouth
I heard once belch sedition from a stall.   35
Go, bear him to the priests; he is a victim
That comes as wished for them, the cooks of heav'n,
And they will carve this brawn of fat rebellion,
As if he were a dish the gods might feed on.

VINDITIUS (*from a window*).

O, the gods! O, the gods! What will they do with him? O   40
these priests, rogues, cutthroats! A dish for the gods, but the
devil's cooks to dress him.

TIBERIUS.

Thus then. The Fecialians have set down
A platform, copied from the king's design.
The Pandane or the Romulide, the Roman,   45
Carmental, and Janiculan Ports of Rome,
The circ, the capitol, and Sublician Bridge
Must all be seized by us that are within.
'Twill not be hard in the surprise of night
By us, the consuls' children and their nephews,   50
To kill the drowsy guards and keep the holds,
At least so long till Tarquin force his entrance
With all the royalists that come to join us.
Therefore, to make his broader squadrons way,

---

29. meetings,] *Q1*; meetings. *Q2,*   *C1–3*.
C1; meetings; *C2–3*.   35. stall.] *C1–3*; stall: *Q1*; stall, *Q2*.
30. forth] *Q1*; forth. *Q2*; forth,

45–47. *The Pandane . . . Bridge*] Stroup and Cooke point out (S-C, II,
594) that the places named here derive from Madeleine de Scudéry's
Clelia, Book II, parts ii and iii.

Tarquinian is designed to be the entry   55
Of his most pompous and resolved revenge.

AQUILIUS.

The first decreed in this great execution
Is here set down your father and Valerius.

TIBERIUS.

That's as the king shall please; but for Valerius,
I'll take myself the honor of his head   60
And wear it on my spear. The senate all
Without exception shall be sacrificed.
And those that are the mutinous heads o' th' people,
Whom I have marked to be the soldiers' spoil,
For plunder must be given, and who so fit   65
As those notorious limbs, your commonwealth's men?
Their daughters to be ravished, and their sons
Quartered like brutes upon the common shambles.

VITELLIUS.

Now for the letters, which the Fecialians
Require us all to sign and send to Tarquin,   70
Who will not else be apt to trust his heralds
Without credentials under every hand,
The business being indeed of vast import,
On which the hazard of his life and empire,
As well as all our fortunes, does depend.   75

TIBERIUS.

It were a break to the whole enterprise
To make a scruple in our great affair;
I will sign first. And for my brother Titus,
Whom his new wife detains, I have his hand
And seal to show, as fast and firm as any.   80

VINDITIUS [*from window*].

O villainy! Villainy! What would they do with me, if they
should catch me peeping? Knock out my brains at least;
another dish for the priests, who would make fine sauce of
'em for the haunch of a fat citizen!

TIBERIUS.

All hands have here subscribed, and that your hearts   85

---

64. soldiers'] soldier's *Q 1*; soldiers
Q 2, C 1-3.

Prove resolute to what your hands have giv'n,
Behold the messengers of heav'n to bind you,
Charms of religion, sacred conjurations,
With sounds of execration, words of horror,
Not to disclose or make least signs or show,   90
Of what you have both heard, and seen, and sworn,
But bear yourselves as if it ne'er had been.
Swear by the gods celestial and infernal,
By Pluto, mother earth, and by the furies,
Not to reveal, though racks were set before you,   95
A syllable of what is past and done.
Hark, how the offered brutes begin to roar!
O that the hearts of all the traitor senate,
And heads of that foul hydra multitude,
Were frying with their fat upon this pile,   100
That we might make an off'ring worth an empire,
And sacrifice rebellion to the king.

The scene draws, showing the sacrifice: one burning and another crucified; the Priests *coming forward with goblets in their hands, filled with human blood.*

FIRST PRIEST.

Kneel all you heroes of this black design,
Each take his goblet filled with blood and wine.
Swear by the thunderer, swear by Jove,   105
Swear by the hundred gods above;
Swear by Dis, by Proserpine,
Swear by the Berecynthian queen.

SECOND PRIEST.

To keep it close till Tarquin comes,
With trumpets' sound and beat of drums;   110
But then to thunder forth the deed,
That Rome may blush and traitors bleed.
Swear all.

89. horror,] *C1–3*; horror *Q1–2*.
97. Hark,] *Q1*; Hark *Q2, C1–3*.
99. of that] *Q1*; of all that *Q2, C1–3*.
108. queen.] *Q1, C3*; queen, *Q2, C1–2*.
110. trumpets'] trumpets *Q1–2*; trumpet *C1–3*.

107. *Dis . . . Proserpine*] deities of the lower world.
108. *Berecynthian queen*] Cybele, known in Rome as mother of the gods.

ALL.   We swear.

FIRST PRIEST.   Now drink the blood
    To make the conjuration good.

TIBERIUS.
    Methinks I feel the slave's exalted blood   115
    Warm at my heart. O that it were the spirits
    Of Rome's best life, drawn from her grizzled fathers!
    That were a draught indeed to quench ambition,
    And give new fierceness to the king's revenge.

VINDITIUS [*from window*].
    O the gods! What, burn a man alive! O cannibals, hell- 120
    hounds! Eat one man and drink another! Well, I'll to
    Valerius; Brutus will not believe me, because his sons and
    nephews are in the business. What, drink a man's blood!
    Roast him and eat him alive! A whole man roasted! Would
    not an ox serve the turn? Priests to do this! O you immortal 125
    gods! For my part, if this be your worship, I renounce you.
    No; if a man can't go to heaven unless your priests eat him
    and drink him and roast him alive, I'll be for the broad way,
    and the devil shall have me at a venture.

                    Enter Titus.

TITUS.
    What ho, Tiberius! Give me back my hand.   130
    What have you done? Horrors and midnight murders!
    The gods, the gods awake you to repentance,
    As they have me. Wouldst thou believe me brother?
    Since I delivered thee that fatal scroll,
    That writing to the king, my heart rebelled   135
    Against itself; my thoughts were up in arms
    All in a roar, like seamen in a storm,
    My reason and my faculties were wracked,
    The mast, the rudder, and the tackling gone;
    My body, like the hull of some lost vessel,   140
    Beaten and tumbled with my rolling fears;

138. wracked,] *Q2, C1–3*; wracked
Q1.

    128–129. *I'll . . . venture.*] an allusion to Matthew 7:13–14.

Therefore I charge thee give me back my writing.

TIBERIUS.

What means my brother?

TITUS.   O Tiberius, O!
Dark as it seems, I tell thee that the gods
Look through a day of lightning on our city.   145
The heav'n's on fire, and from the flaming vault
Portentous blood pours like a torrent down.
There are a hundred gods in Rome tonight,
And every larger spirit is abroad,
Monuments emptied, every urn is shaken   150
To fright the state and put the world in arms.
Just now I saw three Romans stand amazed
Before a flaming sword, then dropped down dead,
Myself untouched; while through the blazing air
A fleeting head, like a full riding moon,   155
Glanced by and cried, "Titus, I am Egeria;
Repent, repent, or certain death attends thee;
Treason and tyranny shall not prevail.
Kingdom shall be no more; Egeria says it.
And that vast turn imperial fate designed   160
I saw, O Titus, on th'eternal loom;
'Tis ripe, 'tis perfect, and is doomed to stand."

FIRST PRIEST.

Fumes, fumes; the phantoms of an ill digestion.
The gods are as good quiet gods as may be,
They're fast asleep and mean not to disturb us,   165
Unless your frenzy wake 'em.

TITUS.   Peace, fury, peace.
May the gods doom me to the pains of hell
If I enjoyed the beauties that I saved.
The horror of my treason shocked my joys,
Enervated my purpose, while I lay   170
Colder than marble by her virgin side,

---

149. every] *Q2, C1–3*; ever *Q1*.   166. Peace, fury, peace.] *C1–3*;
161. loom;] *Q2, C2–3*; loom, *Q1*,   peace fury, peace. *Q1–2*.
C1.

---

156. *Egeria*] goddess of fountains who had counseled Numa; known as a
wise adviser of statesmen.

As if I had drunk the blood of elephants,
Drowsy mandragora, or the juice of hemlock.

FIRST PRIEST.

I like him not; I think we had best dispatch him.

TITUS.

Nothing but images of horror 'round me,   175
Rome all in blood, the ravished vestals raving,
The sacred fire put out; robbed mothers' shrieks
Deaf'ning the gods with clamors for their babes
That sprawled aloft upon the soldiers' spears;
The beard of age plucked off by barbarous hands,   180
While from his piteous wounds and horrid gashes
The laboring life flowed faster than the blood.

Enter Valerius, Vinditius, *with guards, who seize all but the priests, who slip away.* Vinditius *follows them.*

VALERIUS.

Horror upon me! What will this night bring forth?
Yes, you immortal gods, strike, strike the consul.
Since these are here, the crime will look less horrid   185
In me than in his sons. Titus, Tiberius!
O from this time let me be blind and dumb,
But haste there. Mutius, fly; call hither Brutus,
Bid him forever leave the down of rest,
And sleep no more. If Rome were all on fire,   190
And Tarquin in the streets bestriding slaughter,
He would less wonder than at Titus here.

TITUS.

Stop there, O stop that messenger of fate.
Here, bind, Valerius, bind this villain's hands,
Tear off my robes, put me upon the forks,   195

175. me,] *Q1*; me; *Q2, C1–3*.
177. shrieks] *C1–3*; shrieks; *Q1–2*.
178. for] *Q1–2*; from *C1–3*.
179. spears;] *Q2, C1–3*; spears *Q1*.
194. Here, bind,] *Q1, C1–3*; Here, bind *Q2*.
195. robes,] *Q2, C1–3*; robes *Q1*.

172. *drunk . . . elephants*] Stroup and Cooke (S-C, II, 594) call attention to a belief that this would cause impotence.
173. *mandragora*] solution of mandrake root, used as a narcotic.
177. *sacred fire*] fire tended by the Vestal Virgins.
195. *forks*] gallows.

And lash me like a slave till I shall howl
My soul away; or hang me on a cross,
Rack me a year within some horrid dungeon,
So deep, so near the hells that I must suffer,
That I may groan my torments to the damned.   200
I do submit, this traitor, this cursed villain,
To all the stings of most ingenious horror,
So thou dispatch me ere my father comes.
But hark! I hear the tread of fatal Brutus!
By all the gods, and by the lowest furies,   205
I cannot bear his face. Away with me,
Or like a whirlwind I will tear my way
I care not whither.   *Exit with* Tiberius.
VALERIUS.   Take 'em hence together.

Enter Vinditius *with the priests.*

VINDITIUS.
Here, here, my lord, I have unkenneled two.
Those there are rascals made of flesh and blood,   210
Those are but men, but these are the gods' rogues.

VALERIUS.
Go, good Vinditius, haste and stop the people,
Get 'em together to the capitol,
Where all the senate, with the consuls early,
Will see strict justice done upon the traitors.   215
For thee, the senate shall decree rewards
Great as thy service.

VINDITIUS.   I humbly thank your lordship.
[*Aside.*] Why, what, they'll make me a senator at least,
And then a consul. O th'immortal gods!
My lord, I go—[*aside*] to have the rods and axes carried 220
before me and a long purple gown trailing behind my
honorable heels. Well, I am made forever!   *Exit.*

Enter Brutus *attended.*

BRUTUS.
O, my Valerius, are these horrors true?

204. hark!] *Q1;* hark, *Q2, C1–3.*   *C1–3.*
204. Brutus!] *Q1;* Brutus; *Q2,*

Hast thou, O gods, this night emboweled me?
Ransacked thy Brutus' veins, thy fellow consul, 225
And found two villains lurking in my blood?

VALERIUS.
    The blackest treason that e'er darkness brooded.
And who, to hatch these horrors for the world,
Who to seduce the noble youth of Rome,
To draw 'em to so damned a conjuration, 230
To bind 'em too by new invented oaths,
Religious forms, and devilish sacrifices,
A sacrament of blood, for which Rome suffered
In two the worthiest of her martyred sons;
Who to do this, but messengers from heaven? 235
These holy men that swore so solemnly
Before the senate, called the gods to curse 'em,
If they intended aught against the state,
Or harbored treason more than what they uttered?

BRUTUS.
    Now all the fiends and furies thank 'em for it. 240
You sons of murder that get drunk with blood,
Then stab at princes, poison commonwealths,
Destroy whole hecatombs of innocent souls,
Pile 'em like bulls and sheep upon your altars,
As you would smoke the gods from out their dwelling. 245
You shame of earth and scandal of the heav'ns,
You deeper fiends than any of the furies,
That scorn to whisper envy, hate, sedition,
But with a blast of privilege proclaim it;
Priests that are instruments designed to damn us, 250
Fit speaking trumpets for the mouth of hell.
Hence with 'em, guards; secure 'em in the prison
Of Ancus Martius. Read the packets o'er,
I'll bear it as I'm able, read 'em out.

VALERIUS.
    "The sum of the conspiracy to the king. 255
It shall begin with both the consuls' deaths,

255. king.] *Q2, C1–3*; king? *Q1.*

---

224. *emboweled*] from bowel, meaning "children."
253. *Ancus Martius*] fourth king of Rome.

And then the senate; every man must bleed,
But those that have engaged to serve the king.
Be ready therefore, sir, to send your troops
By twelve tomorrow night, and come yourself   260
In person, if you'll reascend the throne.
All that have sworn to serve your majesty
Subscribe themselves by name your faithful subjects:
Tiberius, Aquilius, Vitellius,
Trebonius, Servilius, Minutius,   265
Pomponius, and your Fecialian priests."
BRUTUS.
    Ha! My Valerius, is not Titus there?
VALERIUS.
    He's here, my lord; a paper by itself.
    "Titus to the king.
    Sir, you need only know my brother's mind   270
    To judge of me, who am resolved to serve you."
    What do you think, my lord?
BRUTUS.   Think, my Valerius?
    By my heart, I know not.
    I'm at a loss of thought, and must acknowledge
    The councils of the gods are fathomless;   275
    Nay, 'tis the hardest task perhaps of life
    To be assured of what is vice or virtue.
    Whether when we raise up temples to the gods
    We do not then blaspheme 'em. O, behold me,
    Behold the game that laughing fortune plays;   280
    Fate, or the will of heav'n, call't what you please,
    That mars the best designs that prudence lays,
    That brings events about perhaps to mock
    At human reach, and sport with expectation.
    Consider this, and wonder not at Brutus   285
    If his philosophy seems at a stand,
    If thou behold'st him shed unmanly tears
    To see his blood, his children, his own bowels
    Conspire the death of him that gave 'em being.

272. Valerius?] *Q1*; Valerius! *Q2*,   279. 'em.] 'em *Q1*; 'em: *Q2, C1–3.*
C1–3.

---

284. *reach*] plan, design.

VALERIUS.

    What heart but yours could bear it without breaking?   290

BRUTUS.

    No, my Valerius, I were a beast indeed
    Not to be moved with such prodigious suffering.
    Yet after all I justify the gods,
    And will conclude there's reason supernatural
    That guides us through the world with vast discretion,   295
    Although we have not souls to comprehend it,
    Which makes by wonderous methods the same causes
    Produce effects though of a different nature;
    Since then, for man's instruction, and the glory
    Of the immortal gods, it is decreed   300
    There must be patterns drawn of fiercest virtue,
    Brutus submits to the eternal doom.

VALERIUS.

    May I believe there can be such perfection.
    Such a resolve in man?

BRUTUS.

    First, as I am their father,   305
    I pardon both of 'em this black design;
    But, as I am Rome's consul, I abhor 'em
    And cast 'em from my soul with detestation.
    The nearer to my blood, the deeper grained
    The color of their fault, and they shall bleed.   310
    Yes, my Valerius, both my sons shall die.

Enter Teraminta.

    Nay, I will stand unboweled by the altar,
    See something dearer to me than my entrails
    Displayed before the gods and Roman people,
    The sacrifice of justice and revenge.   315

TERAMINTA.

    What sacrifice, what victims, sir, are these
    Which you intend? O, you eternal powers,
    How shall I vent my sorrows! O, my lord,
    Yet ere you seal the death you have designed,

298. effects] *Q1*; effects, *Q2, C1–3.*   nature. *C2–3.*
298. nature;] *Q2, C1*; nature, *Q1*;   301. virtue,] *C1–3*; virtue; *Q1–2.*

The death of all that's lovely in the world,   320
Hear what the witness of his soul can say,
The only evidence that can, or dare,
Appear for your unhappy, guiltless son.
The gods command you; virtue, truth, and justice,
Which you with so much rigor have adored,   325
Beg you would hear the wretched Teraminta.

BRUTUS.

Cease thy laments. Though of the blood of Tarquin,
Yet more, the wife of my forgotten son,
Thou shalt be heard.

TERAMINTA.   Have you forgot him then?
Have you forgot your self? The image of you,   330
The very picture of your excellence,
The portraiture of all your manly virtues,
Your visage stamped upon him. Just those eyes,
The moving greatness of 'em, all the mercy,
The shedding goodness; not so quite severe,   335
Yet still most like. And can you then forget him?

BRUTUS.

Will you proceed?

TERAMINTA.   My lord, I will. Know then,
After your son, your son that loves you more
Than I love him, after our common Titus,
The wealth o' th' world unless you rob 'em of it,   340
Had long endured th'assaults of the rebellious,
And still kept fixed to what you had enjoined him;
I, as fate ordered it, was sent from Tullia,
With my death menaced, ev'n before his eyes,
Doomed to be stabbed before him by the priests,   345
Unless he yielded not t'oppose the king.
Consider, sir. O make it your own case;
Just wedded, just on the expected joys,
Warm for my bed, and rushing to my arms,
So loving too, alas, as we did love.   350
Granted in haste, in heat, in flame of passion
He knew not what himself, and so subscribed.

346. king.] king: *Q2, C1–3*; king,
Q1.

But now, sir, now, my lord, behold a wonder,
Behold a miracle to move your soul!
Though in my arms, just in the grasps of pleasure,   355
His noble heart, struck with the thoughts of Brutus,
Of what he promised you, till then forgot,
Leaped in his breast and dashed him from enjoyment;
He shrieked, "Y'immortal gods, what have I done!
No, Teraminta, let us rather perish,   360
Divide forever with whole seas betwixt us,
Rather than sin against so good a father."
Though he before had barred your life and fortune,
Yet would not trust the traitors with the safety
Of him he called the image of the gods.   365

VALERIUS.

O saint-like virtue of a Roman wife!
O eloquence divine! Now all the arts
Of women's tongues, the rhetoric of the gods,
Inspire thy soft and tender soul to move him.

TERAMINTA.

On this he roused. Swore by the powers divine,   370
He would fetch back the paper that he gave,
Or leave his life amongst 'em. Kept his word,
And came to challenge it, but, O, too late;
For in the midst of all his piety,
His strong persuasions to a swift repentance,   375
His vows to lay their horrid treasons open,
His execration of the barbarous priests,
How he abhorred that bloody sacrament
As much as you, and cursed the conjuration;
Vinditius came that had before alarmed   380
The wise Valerius, who with all the guards
Found Titus here, believed him like the rest,
And seized him too, as guilty of the treason.

VALERIUS.

But, by the gods, my soul does now acquit him.
Blest be thy tongue, blest the auspicious gods   385
That sent thee, O true pattern of perfection,
To plead his bleeding cause. There needs no more;

356. heart,] *Q2, C1–3*; heart *Q1*.

I see his father's moved. Behold a joy,
A wat'ry comfort rising in his eyes,
That says, "'Tis more than half a heav'n to hear thee."   390

BRUTUS.

Haste, O Valerius, haste and send for Titus.

TERAMINTA.

For Titus! O, that is a word too distant;
Say, for your son, for your beloved son,
The darling of the world, the joy of heav'n,
The hope of earth, your eyes not dearer to you,   395
Your soul's best wish, and comfort of your age.

Enter Titus *with* Valerius.

TITUS.

Ah, sir! O whither shall I run to hide me?
Where shall I lower fall? How shall I lie
More groveling in your view and howl for mercy?
Yet 'tis some comfort to my wild despair,   400
Some joy in death that I may kiss your feet,
And swear upon 'em by these streaming tears,
Black as I am with all my guilt upon me,
I never harbored aught against your person.
Ev'n in the height of my full fraught distraction,   405
Your life, my lord, was sacred; ever dear,
And ever precious, to unhappy Titus.

BRUTUS.

Rise, Titus. Rise, my son.

TITUS.   Alas, I dare not;
I have not strength to see the majesty
Which I have braved. If thus far I aspire,   410
If on your knees I hang and vent my groans,
It is too much, too much for thousand lives.

BRUTUS.

I pity thee, my son, and I forgive thee.
And that thou mayst believe my mercy true,
I take thee in my arms.

TITUS.   O all the gods!   415

BRUTUS.

Now rise; I charge thee, on my blessing, rise.

408. Rise,] *Q2, C1–3*; Rise *Q1.*

TERAMINTA.

 Ah! See, sir, see, against his will behold
 He does obey, though he would choose to kneel
 An age before you; see how he stands and trembles!
 Now, by my hopes of mercy, he's so lost,   420
 His heart's so full, brimful of tenderness,
 The sense of what you've done has struck him speechless;
 Nor can he thank you now but with his tears.

BRUTUS.

 My dear Valerius, let me now entreat thee
 Withdraw a while with gentle Teraminta,   425
 And leave us to ourselves.

TERAMINTA.

 Ah, sir, I fear you now;
 Nor can I leave you with the humble Titus,
 Unless you promise me you will not chide,
 Nor fall again to anger. Do not, sir,   430
 Do not upbraid his soft and melting temper
 With what is past. Behold he sighs again!
 Now by the gods that hitherto have blessed us,
 My heart forebodes a storm, I know not why.
 But say, my lord; give me your godlike word 435
 You'll not be cruel, and I'll not trust my heart,
 Howe'er it leaps and fills me with new horror.

BRUTUS.

 I promise thee.

TERAMINTA.   Why, then I thank you, sir;
 Ev'n from my soul I thank you for this goodness.
 The great, good, gracious gods reward and bless you. 440
 Ah Titus, ah my soul's eternal treasure,
 I fear I leave thee with a hard usurer;
 But I perforce must trust thee. O farewell.

          Exit with Valerius.

BRUTUS.

 Well Titus, speak; how is it with thee now?
 I would attend awhile this mighty motion, 445
 Wait till the tempest were quite overblown,
 That I might take thee in the calm of nature,

446. overblown] *C1–3*; o'verblown
Q1; o'erblown *Q2*.

With all thy gentler virtues brooding on thee,
So hushed a stillness, as if all the gods
Looked down and listened to what we were saying.   450
Speak then and tell me, O my best beloved,
My son, my Titus, is all well again?

TITUS.

So well that saying how must make it nothing;
So well that I could wish to die this moment,
For so my heart with powerful throbs persuades me.   455
That were indeed to make you reparation,
That were, my lord, to thank you home, to die,
And that for Titus too would be most happy.

BRUTUS.

How's that, my son? Would death for thee be happy?

TITUS.

Most certain, sir. For in my grave I scape   460
All those affronts which I in life must look for,
All those reproaches which the eyes and fingers
And tongues of Rome will daily cast upon me,
From whom, to a soul so sensible as mine,
Each single scorn would be far worse than dying.   465
Besides, I scape the stings of my own conscience,
Which will forever rack me with remembrance,
Haunt me by day and torture me by night,
Casting my blotted honor in the way
Where'er my melancholy thoughts shall guide me.   470

BRUTUS.

But is not death a very dreadful thing?

TITUS.

Not to a mind resolved. No, sir, to me
It seems as natural as to be born.
Groans and convulsions and discolored faces,
Friends weeping round us, blacks and obsequies   475
Make it a dreadful thing; the pomp of death
Is far more terrible than death itself.
Yes, sir; I call the powers of heav'n to witness,

457. die,] *Q2, C1–3*; die *Q1*.   478. sir;] *Q1*; sir, *Q2, C1–3*.

472–477. *to me . . . death itself.*] As Stroup and Cooke note (S-C, II, 595),
this passage owes much to Bacon's essay "Of Death."

Titus dares die if so you have decreed;
Nay, he shall die with joy to honor Brutus,   480
To make your justice famous through the world
And fix the liberty of Rome forever.
Not but I must confess my weakness too;
Yet it is great thus to resolve against it,
To have the frailty of a mortal man,   485
But the security of th'immortal gods.

BRUTUS.

O Titus, O thou absolute young man!
Thou flatt'ring mirror of thy father's image,
Where I behold myself at such advantage!
Thou perfect glory of the Junian race!   490
Let me endear thee once more to my bosom,
Groan an eternal farewell to thy soul;
Instead of tears weep blood if possible,
Blood, the heart blood of Brutus, on his child,
For thou must die, my Titus, die, my son,   495
I swear the gods have doomed thee to the grave.
The violated genius of thy country
Rears his sad head and passes sentence on thee.
This morning sun, that lights my sorrows on
To the tribunal of this horrid vengeance,   500
Shall never see thee more.

TITUS.   Alas, my lord!
Why are you moved thus? Why am I worth your sorrow?
Why should the godlike Brutus shake to doom me?
Why all these trappings for a traitor's hearse?
The gods will have it so.

BRUTUS.   They will, my Titus;   505
Nor heav'n, nor earth can have it otherwise.
Nay, Titus, mark; the deeper that I search,
My harassed soul returns the more confirmed.
Methinks I see the very hand of Jove
Moving the dreadful wheels of this affair   510
That whirl thee, like a machine, to thy fate.

487. Titus,] *Q1*; Titus! *Q2, C1–3*.   496. grave.] grave, *Q1–2*; grave:
C1–3.

---

490. *Junian*] adjective derived from *Junius*.

It seems as if the gods had preordained it
To fix the reeling spirits of the people
And settle the loose liberty of Rome.
'Tis fixed. O therefore let not fancy fond thee.   515
So fixed thy death that 'tis not in the power
Of gods or men to save thee from the axe.

TITUS.

The axe! O heav'n! Then must I fall so basely?
What, shall I perish by the common hangman?

BRUTUS.

If thou deny me this, thou givest me nothing.   520
Yes, Titus, since the gods have so decreed
That I must lose thee, I will take th'advantage
Of thy important fate, cement Rome's flaws,
And heal her wounded freedom with thy blood.
I will ascend myself the sad tribunal,   525
And sit upon my sons; on thee, my Titus;
Behold thee suffer all the shame of death,
The lictor's lashes, bleed before people;
Then, with thy hopes and all thy youth upon thee,
See thy head taken by the common axe,   530
Without a groan, without one pitying tear,
If that the gods can hold me to my purpose,
To make my justice quite transcend example.

TITUS.

Scourged like a bondman! Ha! A beaten slave!
But I deserve it all; yet here I fail.   535
The image of this suff'ring quite unmans me,
Nor can I longer stop the gushing tears.
O sir! O Brutus! Must I call you father,
Yet have no token of your tenderness,
No sign of mercy? What, not bate me that!   540
Can you resolve, O all th'extremity
Of cruel rigor, to behold me too,

---

519. What,] *Q2, C1–3*; What *Q1.*   528. before people] *Q1–2, C1*;
519. hangman] *Q1, C1–3*; hangmen   before the people *C2–3.*
Q2.

---

515. *fond*] "make a fool of" (*OED*).

To sit unmoved and see me whipped to death?
Where are your bowels now? Is this a father?
Ah, sir, why should you make my heart suspect   545
That all your late compassion was dissembled?
How can I think that you did ever love me?

BRUTUS.

Think that I love thee by my present passion,
By these unmanly tears, these earthquakes here,
These sighs that twitch the very strings of life.   550
Think that no other cause on earth could move me
To tremble thus, to sob, or shed a tear,
Nor shake my solid virtue from her point
But Titus' death. O do not call it shameful,
That thus shall fix the glory of the world.   555
I own thy suff'rings ought t'unman me thus,
To make me throw my body on the ground,
To bellow like a beast, to gnaw the earth,
To tear my hair, to curse the cruel fates
That force a father thus to drag his bowels.   560

TITUS.

O rise, thou violated majesty,
Rise from the earth, or I shall beg those fates
Which you would curse to bolt me to the center.
I now submit to all your threatened vengeance.
Come forth, you executioners of justice,   565
Nay, all you lictors, slaves, and common hangmen,
Come, strip me bare, unrobe me in his sight,
And lash me till I bleed; whip me like furies;
And when you've scourged me till I foam and fall,
For want of spirits groveling in the dust,   570
Then take my head and give it his revenge.
By all the gods I greedily resign it.

BRUTUS.

No more, farewell, eternally farewell.
If there be gods they will reserve a room,
A throne for thee in heav'n. One last embrace.   575
What is it makes thy eyes thus swim again?

---

566. Nay,] *Q2, C1–3*; Nay *Q1*.   569. you've] *C1–3*; you'have *Q1–2*.
568. bleed;] *Q1*; bleed, *Q2, C1–3*.

TITUS.

>   I had forgot. Be good to Teraminta
>   When I am ashes.

BRUTUS.   Leave her to my care.

>   See her thou must not, for thou canst not bear it.
>   O for one more, this pull, this tug of heartstrings.   580
>   Farewell forever.

TITUS.   O Brutus! O my father!

BRUTUS.

>   Canst thou not say farewell?

TITUS.   Farewell forever.

BRUTUS.

>   Forever then. But, O, my tears run o'er.
>   Groans choke my words, and I can speak no more.   *Exeunt.*

ACT V

[V.i]   [*Enter*] Valerius, Horatius, Herminius, Mutius.

HORATIUS.

   His sons condemned?

VALERIUS.   Doomed to the rods and axes.

HORATIUS.

   What, both of 'em?

VALERIUS.   Both, sir, both, both his sons.

HORATIUS.

   What, Titus too?

VALERIUS.   Yes, sir, his darling Titus.

   Nay, though he knows him innocent as I am,

   'Tis all one, sir, his sentence stands like fate.   5

HORATIUS.

   Yet I'll entreat him.

MUTIUS.   So will I.

HERMINIUS.   And I.

VALERIUS.

   Entreat him! Yes, you may, my lords, and move him

   As I have done. Why, he's no more a man;

   He is not cast in the same common mold,

   His spirit moves not with our springs and wards.   10

   He looks and talks as if that Jove had sent him

   To be the judge of all the under world;

   Tells me, this palace of the universe,

   With that vast moat, the ocean, running round us,

   Th'eternal stars so fiercely rolling o'er us,   15

   With all that circulation of heav'n's orbs,

   Were so established from before all ages

   To be the dowry of majestic Rome;

   Then looks as if he had a patent for it

   To take account of all this great expense,   20

   And see the layings out of the round world.

HERMINIUS.

   What shall be done then? For it grieves my soul

   To think of Titus' loss.

VALERIUS.   There is no help,

   But thus to shake your head and cross your arms

---

2. What,] *C1–3*; What *Q1–2*.   14. ocean,] *Q1*; ocean *Q2, C1–3*.

And wonder what the gods and he intend.   25

HERMINIUS.

There's scarce one man of this conspiracy
But is some way related, if not nearly,
To Junius Brutus. Some of the Aquilians
Are nephews to him, and Vitellius' sister,
The grave Sempronia, is the consul's wife.   30

VALERIUS.

Therefore, I have engaged that groaning matron
To plead the cause of her unhappy sons.

Enter Titus *with lictors.*

But see, O gods, behold the gallant Titus,
The mirror of all sons, the white of virtue,
Filled up with blots and writ all o'er with blood,   35
Bowing with shame his body to the ground,
Whipped out of breath by these inhuman slaves!
O, Titus! Is this possible? This shame?

TITUS.

O, my Valerius, call it not my shame;
By all the gods, it is to Titus honor,   40
My constant suff'rings are my only glory.
What have I left besides? But ask, Valerius,
Ask these good men that have performed their duty,
If all the while they whipped me like a slave,
If when the blood from every part ran down,   45
I gave one groan or shed a woman's tear.
I think, I swear, I think, O my Valerius,
That I have borne it well, and like a Roman.
But, O, far better shall I bear my death,
Which, as it brings less pain, has less dishonor.   50

Enter Teraminta *wounded.*

TERAMINTA.

Where is he? Where, where is this godlike son
Of an inhuman, barbarous, bloody father?

27. related,] *Q2, C1–3*; related *Q1*.   *C2–3.*
34. virtue,] *Q2, C1–3*; virtue; *Q1.*   42. ask,] *C1–3*; ask *Q1–2.*
40. Titus] *Q1–2*; Titus, *C1*; Titus'

O bear me to him.
TITUS.   Ha! My Teraminta!
Is't possible? The very top of beauty,
This perfect face drawn by the gods at council,   55
Which they were long a-making, as they had reason,
For they shall never hit the like again,
Defiled and mangled thus! What barbarous wretch
Has thus blasphemed this bright original?
TERAMINTA.
For me it matters not, nor my abuses;   60
But, O, for thee, why have they used thee thus?
Whipped, Titus, whipped! And could the gods look on?
The glory of the world thus basely used?
Lashed, whipped, and beaten by these upright dogs,
Whose souls, with all the virtue of the senate,   65
Will be but foils to any fault of thine,
Who hast a beauty ev'n in thy offending.
And did thy father doom thee thus? O Titus,
Forgive thy dying part, if she believes
A wretch so barbarous never could produce thee.   70
Some god, some god, my Titus, watched his absence,
Slipped to thy mother's bed and gave thee to the world.
TITUS.
O this last wound, this stab to all my courage!
Hadst thou been well, I could have borne more lashes.
And is it thus my father does protect thee?   75
TERAMINTA.
Ah Titus! What, thy murd'rer my protector!
No, let me fall again among the people,
Let me be hooted like a common strumpet,
Tossed, as I was, and dragged about the streets,
The bastard of a Tarquin, foiled in dirt,   80
The cry of all those bloodhounds that did hunt me
Thus to the goal of death, this happy end
Of all my miseries, here to pant my last,
To wash thy gashes with my farewell tears,
To murmur, sob, and lean my aching head   85

---

65. senate,] *Q2, C1–3*; senate *Q1*.   67. ev'n] *Q1*; e'en *Q2, C1–3*.

80. *foiled*] polluted.

Upon thy breast, thus like a cradle babe
To suck thy wounds and bubble out my soul.

Enter Sempronia, Aquilia, Vitellia, *mourners, etc.*

SEMPRONIA.
Come ladies, haste, and let us to the senate;
If the gods give us leave, we'll be today
Part of the council. O, my son, my Titus!   90
See here the bloody justice of a father,
See how the vengeance rains from his own bowels!
Is he not mad? If he refuse to hear us,
We'll bind his hands as one bereft of reason.
Haste then. O Titus, I would stay to moan thee,   95
But that I fear his orders are gone out
For something worse, for death, to take the heads
Of all the kindred of these wretched women.

TERAMINTA.
Come then. I think I have some spirits left
To join thee, O most pious, best of mothers,   100
To melt this rocky heart. Give me your hand;
Thus let us march before this wretched host
And offer to that god of blood our vows.
If there be aught that's human left about him,
Perhaps my wounds and horrible abuses,   105
Helped with the tears and groans of this sad troop,
May batter down the best of his resolves.

TITUS.
Hark, Teraminta.

TERAMINTA.   No, my lord, away.   [*Women*] *exeunt.*

TITUS.
O, my Valerius! Was there ever day
Through all the legends of recorded time   110
So sad as this? But see, my father comes!

Enter Brutus, Tiberius, *lictors.*

Tiberius too has undergone the lash.
Give him the patience, gods, of martyred Titus,

86. thus] *Q1*; thus, *Q2, C1–3*.   *C1–3.*
86. babe] *Q1*; babe, *Q2, C1–3*.   106. troop,] *Q2, C1–3*; troop *Q1*.
99. then.] then: *Q1*; then, *Q2,*

And he will bless those hands that have chastised him.

TIBERIUS.

 Enjoy the bloody conquest of thy pride,   115
 Thou more tyrannical than any Tarquin,
 Thou fiercer sire of these unhappy sons
 Than impious Saturn or the gorged Thyestes.
 This cormorant sees and owns us for his children,
 Yet preys upon his entrails, tears his bowels   120
 With thirst of blood and hunger fetched from hell,
 Which famished Tantalus would start to think on.
 But end, barbarian, end the horrid vengeance
 Which thou so impiously hast begun,
 Perfect thy justice, as thou, tyrant, call'st it,   125
 Sit like a fury on thy black tribunal,
 Grasp with thy monstrous hands these gory heads,
 And let thy flatt'ring orators adore thee
 For triumphs which shall make thee smile at horror.

BRUTUS.

 Lead to the senate.

TIBERIUS.   Go then to the senate,   130
 There make thy boast how thou hast doomed thy children
 To forks and whips, for which the gods reward thee.
 Away. My spirit scorns more conference with thee.
 The axe will be as laughter; but the whips
 That drew these stains, for this I beg the gods   135
 With my last breath, for every drop that falls
 From these vile wounds, to thunder curses on thee. *Exit.*

BRUTUS.

 Valerius, haste; the senate does attend us.   *Exit.*

TITUS.

 Valerius, ere you go, let me conjure thee,
 By all the earth holds great or honorable,   140
 As thou art truly Roman, stamped a man,
 Grant to thy dying Titus one request.

VALERIUS.

 I'll grant thee anything, but do not talk

139. thee,] *C1–3*; thee *Q1–2*.

---

118. *Saturn . . . Thyestes.*] Both of these mythological figures devoured their own children.

Of dying yet; for much I dare confide
In that sad company that's gone before.   145
I know they'll move him to preserve his Titus,
For, though you marked him not, as hence he parted
I could perceive with joy a silent shower
Run down his silver beard. Therefore have hope.

TITUS.

Hope, say'st thou! O the gods! What hope of life?   150
To live, to live! And after this dishonor!
No, my Valerius, do not make me rave;
But if thou hast a soul that's sensible,
Let me conjure thee, when we reach the senate,
To thrust me through the heart.

VALERIUS.   Not for the world.   155

TITUS.

Do't, or I swear thou hast no friendship for me.
First, thou wilt save me from the hated axe,
The hangman's hand; for by the gods I tell thee
Thou mayst as well stop the eternal sun,
And drive him back, as turn my father's purpose.   160
Next, and what most my soul entreats thee for,
I shall perhaps in death procure his pity;
For to die thus, beneath his killing frown,
Is damning me before my execution.

VALERIUS.

'Tis granted. By the gods, I swear to end thee;   165
For when I weigh with my more serious thought
Thy father's conduct in this dreadful justice,
I find it is impossible to save thee.
Come then, I'll lead thee, O thou glorious victim,
Thus to the altar of untimely death,   170
Thus in thy trim, with all thy bloom of youth,
These virtues on thee, whose eternal spring
Shall blossom on thy monumental marble
With never fading glory.

TITUS.   Let me clasp thee,

152. No,] *Q2, C1–3*; No *Q1*.   172. These] *Q2, C1–3*; This *Q1*.
165. thee;] *Q2, C1–3*; thee *Q1*.

144. *confide*] "trust or have faith" (*OED*).

Boil out my thanks thus with my farewell spirits.   175
And now away, the taper's almost out,
Never, Valerius, to be kindled more!
Or, if it be, my friend, it shall continue,
Burn through all winds against the puff of fortune
To dazzle still and shine like the fixed stars,   180
With beams of glory that shall last forever.   *Exeunt.*

Scena ultima.

[V.ii]   <center>*Senate.*</center>

BRUTUS.

Health to the senate! To the fathers hail!
Jupiter, Horscius, and Diespiter,
Hospital and Feretrian, Jove the stayer,
With all the hundred gods and goddesses,
Guard and defend the liberty of Rome.   5
It has been found a famous truth in story,
Left by the ancient sages to their sons,
That on the change of empires or of kingdoms,
Some sudden execution, fierce and great,
Such as may draw the world to admiration,   10
Is necessary to be put in act
Against the enemies of the present state.
Had Hector, with the Greeks and Trojans met
Upon the truce and mingled with each other,
Brought to the banquet of those demigods   15
The fatal head of that illustrious whore,
Troy might have stood till now; but that was wanting.
Jove having from eternity set down
Rome to be head of all the under world,
Raised with this thought, and big with prophecy   20
Of what vast good may grow by such examples,
Brutus stands forth to do a dreadful justice.

176–177.] To lose the light of this   178. be,] *Q2, C1–3*; be *Q1.*
dear world for ever! *mistakenly in-*   [V.ii]
serted between these two lines in C1–3.   19. world,] *Q1–2*; world. *C1–3.*
Cf. V.ii.71.

2–3. *Jupiter . . . stayer*] All are names and titles applied to Jupiter.

I come, O conscript fathers, to a deed
Wholly portentous, new, and wonderful,
Such as, perhaps, has never yet been found   25
In all memorials of former ages,
Nor ever will again. My sons are traitors,
Their tongues and hands are witnesses confessed;
Therefore I have already passed their sentence,
And wait with you to see their execution.   30

HORATIUS.

Consul, the senate does not ask their deaths.
They are content with what's already done,
And all entreat you to remit the axe.

BRUTUS.

I thank you, fathers, but refuse the offer.
By the assaulted majesty of Rome,   35
I swear there is no way to quit the grace,
To right the commonwealth and thank the gods,
But by the sacrificing of my bowels.
Take then, you sad revengers of the public,
These traitors hence; strike off their heads, and then   40
My sons'. No more; their doom is passed. Away.
Thus shall we stop the mouth of loud sedition,
Thus show the difference betwixt the sway
Of partial tyrants and of a freeborn people,
Where no man shall offend because he's great,   45
Where none need doubt his wife's or daughter's honor,
Where all enjoy their own without suspicion,
Where there's no innovation of religion,
No change of laws, nor breach of privilege,
No desperate factions gaping for rebellion,   50
No hopes of pardon for assassinates,
No rash advancements of the base or stranger,
For luxury, for wit, or glorious vice;
But on the contrary, a balanced trade,
Patriots encouraged, manufactors cherished,   55

46. wife's] *Q2, C1–3*; wives *Q1*.   factures *C2–3*.
55. manufactors] *Q1–2, C1*; manu-

---

23. *conscript fathers*] "collective title by which the Roman senators were addressed" (*OED*).
36. *quit the grace*] pay the debt.

Vagabonds, walkers, drones, and swarming braves,
The froth of states, scummed from the commonwealth,
Idleness banished, all excess repressed,
And riots checked by sumptuary laws.
O, conscript fathers, 'tis on these foundations   60
That Rome shall build her empire to the stars,
Send her commanders with her armies forth
To tame the world and give the nations law,
Consuls, proconsuls, who to the capitol
Shall ride upon the necks of conquered kings;   65
And when they die, mount from the gorgeous pile
In flames of spice and mingle with the gods.

HORATIUS.

Excellent Brutus! All the senate thanks thee,
And says that thou thyself art half a god.

Enter Sempronia, Teraminta, *with the rest of the mourners;* Titus,
Valerius, Junius.

SEMPRONIA.

Gone, gone to death! Already sentenced! Doomed!   70
To lose the light of this dear world forever!
What, my Tiberius too! Ah, barbarous! Brutus!
Send, haste, revoke the order of their fate.
By all the pledges of our marriage bed,
If thou, inhuman judge, hast left me one   75
To put thee yet in mind thou art a father;
Speak to him, O you mothers of sad Rome,
Sisters and daughters, ere the execution
Of all your blood; haste, haste, and run about him,
Groan, sob, howl out the terrors of your souls,   80
Nay, fly upon him like robbed savages,
And tear him for your young.

57. commonwealth,] *Q2, C1*; commonwealth: *Q1*; commonwealth;
C2–3.
58. banished,] *Q2, C1–3*; banished
Q1.
60. fathers,] *Q1*; fathers! *Q2, C1–3*.
63. law,] *Q1*; law; *Q2, C1–3*.
65. kings;] *Q1*; kings, *Q2, C1–3*.

71. To lose . . . forever?] *Q1*; To
lose . . . for ever! *Q2*; *om. C1–3*. Cf.
V.i.176–177.
72. barbarous!] *Q1*; barbarous *Q2,
C1–3*.
79. blood;] *Q2, C1–3*; blood, *Q1*.
82. for] *Q1–2*; from *C1–3*.

BRUTUS.   Away, and leave me.

SEMPRONIA.

    Or if you think it better for your purpose,

    Because he has the pow'r of life and death,

    Entreat him thus. Throw all your heartless breasts   85

    Low at his feet and like a god adore him;

    Nay, make a rampier round him with your bodies

    And block him up. I see he would be going;

    Yet that's a sign that our complaints have moved him.

    Continued falls of ever streaming tears,   90

    Such, and so many, and the chastest too

    Of all the pious matrons throughout Rome,

    Perhaps may melt this adamantine temper.

    Not yet! Nay, hang your bodies then upon him,

    Some on his arms, and some upon his knees,   95

    And lay this innocent about his neck,

    This little smiling image of his father.

    See how he bends, and stretches to his bosom!

    O all you pitying pow'rs, the darling weeps;

    His pretty eyes ruddy and wet with tears,   100

    Like two burst cherries rolling in a storm,

    Plead for our griefs more than a thousand tongues.

JUNIUS.

    Yes, yes, my father will be good to us,

    And spare my brothers; O, I know he will.

    Why, do you think he ever was in earnest?   105

    What, to cut off their heads? I warrant you

    He will not; no, he only meant to fright 'em,

    As he will me, when I have done a fault.

    Why, mother, he has whipped 'em for't already,

    And do you think he has the heart to kill 'em?   110

    No, no, he would not cut their little fingers

    For all the world; or if he should, I'm sure

    The gods would pay him for't.

BRUTUS.   What ho! Without there!

    Slaves, villains, ha! Are not my orders heard?

99. pow'rs, the] *C1–3*; pow'rs of the
Q1–2.

---

    87. *rampier*] rampart.

HORATIUS.

    O Brutus, see, they are too well performed!   115
    See here the bodies of the Roman youth
    All headless by your doom, and there Tiberius.

TERAMINTA.

    See, sir, behold, is not this horrid slaughter,
    This cutting off one limb from your own body,
    Is't not enough? O, will it not suffice   120
    To stop the mouth of the most bloody law?
    O, it were highest sin to make a doubt,
    To ask you now to save the innocent Titus,
    The common wish and general petition
    Of all the Roman senate, matrons, wives,   125
    Widows, and babes; nay, ev'n the madding people
    Cry out at last that treason is revenged,
    And ask no more. O, therefore spare him, sir.

BRUTUS.

    I must not hear you. Hark, Valerius.

TERAMINTA.

    By all these wounds upon my virgin breast,   130
    Which I have suffered by your cruelty,
    Although you promised Titus to defend me.

SEMPRONIA.

    Yet hold thy bloody hand, tyrannic Brutus,
    And I'll forgive thee for that headless horror.
    Grant me my Titus, O in death I ask thee.   135
    Thou hast already broke Sempronia's heart;
    Yet I will pardon that, so Titus live.
    Ah, cruel judge! Thou pitiless avenger!
    What art thou whisp'ring? Speak the horror out,
    For in thy glaring eyes I read a murder.   140

BRUTUS.

    I charge thee, by thy oath, Valerius,
    As thou art here deputed by the gods,
    And not a subject for a woman's folly,
    Take him away, and drag him to the axe.

126. ev'n] *Q1*; e'en *Q2, C1–3*.   135. thee.] *Q2, C1–3*; thee, *Q1*.
128. sir.] *Q1*; sir! *Q2, C1–3*.   140. glaring] *C2–3*; glaving *Q1–2,*
129. you.] you, *Q1*; you: *Q2, C1–3*.   *C1*.

VALERIUS.

    It shall be thus then; not the hangman's hand.   145

          Runs him through. The women shriek.

TITUS.

    O bravely struck! Thou hast hit me to the earth
    So nobly, that I shall rebound to heav'n,
    Where I will thank thee for this gallant wound.

            Sempronia *swoons.*

BRUTUS.

    Take hence this woman; haste, and bear her home.
    Why, my Valerius, didst thou rob my justice?   150

TITUS.

    I wrought him to it, sir, that thus in death
    I might have leave to pay my last obedience,
    And beg your blessing for the other world.

TERAMINTA.

    O do not take it, Titus; whate'er comes
    From such a monstrous nature must be blasting.   155
    Ah, thou inhuman tyrant! But, alas,
    I loiter here when Titus stays for me.
    Look here, my love; thou shalt not be before me.

            Stabs herself.

    Thus, to thy arms then. O, make haste, my Titus,
    I'm got already in the grove of death;   160
    The heav'n is all benighted, not one star
    To light us through the dark and pathless maze.
    I have lost thy spirit; O, I grope about
    But cannot find thee. Now I sink in shadows.   *Dies.*

TITUS.

    I come, thou matchless virtue. O, my heart!   165
    Farewell, my love; we'll meet in heav'n again.
    My lord, I hope your justice is atoned;
    I hope the glorious liberty of Rome,
    Thus watered by the blood of both your sons,
    Will get imperial growth and flourish long.   170

150. justice?] *Q2, C1–3;* justice:
Q1.

BRUTUS.

    Thou hast so nobly borne thyself in dying,
    That not to bless thee were to curse myself;
    Therefore I give thee thus my last embrace,
    Print this last kiss upon thy trembling lips.
    And, ere thou goest, I beg thee to report me   175
    To the great shades of Romulus and Numa,
    Just with that majesty and rugged virtue
    Which they inspired and which the world has seen.
    So, for I see thou'rt gone, farewell forever.
    Eternal Jove, the king of gods and men,   180
    Reward and crown thee in the other world.

TITUS.

    What happiness has life to equal this?
    By all the gods I would not live again;
    For what can Jove or all the gods give more,
    To fall thus crowned with virtue's fullest charms,   185
    And die thus blessed in such a father's arms?   *Dies.*

VALERIUS.

    He's gone; the gallant spirit's fled forever.
    How fares this noble vessel, that is robbed
    Of all its wealth, spoiled of its top-mast glory,
    And now lies floating in this world of ruin?   190

BRUTUS.

    Peace, consul, peace; let us not soil the pomp
    Of this majestic fate with woman's brawls.
    Kneel fathers, friends, kneel all you Roman people,
    Hushed as dead calms, while I conceive a pray'r
    That shall be worthy Rome, and worthy Jove.   195

VALERIUS.

    Inspire him, gods; and thou, O Rome, attend.

BRUTUS.

    Let heav'n and earth forever keep their bound,
    The stars unshaken go their constant round;
    In harmless labor be our steel employed,
    And endless peace through all the world enjoyed;   200

184. more,] *Q2, C1–3*; more: *Q1.*   200. enjoyed;] enjoy'd, *Q1*; en-
189. top-mast] *Q1*; topmost *Q2,*   joy'd: *Q2, C1–3.*
C1–3.

Let every bark the waves in safety plough,
No angry tempest curl the ocean's brow;
No darted flames from heav'n make mortals fear,
Nor thunder fright the weeping passenger;
Let not poor swains for storms at harvest mourn,   205
But smile to see their hoards of bladed corn;
No dreadful comets threaten from the skies,
No venom fall, nor pois'nous vapors rise.
Thou, Jove, who dost the fates of empires doom,
Guard and defend the liberty of Rome.   210

FINIS

EPILOGUE

Spoken by Mrs. Barry

No cringing sirs, the poet's champion I
Have sworn to stand and ev'ry judge defy;
But why each bullying critic should I name
A judge, whose only business is to damn;
While you your arbitrary fist advance   5
At wit, and dust it like a boor of France,
Who without show of reason or pretense
Condemn a man to die for speaking sense?
Howe'er we termed you once the wise, the strong,
Know we have borne your impotence too long.   10
You that above your sires presume to soar,
And are but copies daubed in miniature;
You that have nothing right in heart nor tongue
But only to be resolute in wrong;
Who sense affect with such an awkward air   15
As if a Frenchman should become severe;
Or an Italian make his wife a jest,
Like Spaniards pleasant, or like Dutchmen dressed;
That rank the noblest poets with the vile
And look yourselves in a plebeian style.   20
But with an oath—
False as your wit and judgment now I swear
By the known maidenheads of each theater;
Nay, by my own; the poets shall not stand,
Like Shrovetide cocks, the palt of every hand.   25
Let not the purblind critic's sentence pass
That shoots the poet through an optic glass,
No peals of ill-placed praise from galleries come,
Nor punk below to clap or hiss presume;
Let her not cackle at the fops that flout her;   30

Mrs. Barry] Mr. Barrey *Q1–2*;   *C1–3.*
Mrs. Barrey *C1–3.*   8. sense?] sense. *Q1*; sense; *Q2*,
1. sirs] *Q1, C1–3*; sir *Q2*.   *C1–3.*
4. damn;] damn. *Q1*; damn? *Q2*, 30. at the] *Q1–2, C1*; as the *C2–3.*

---

25. *Shrovetide cocks*] "a cock tied up and pelted with sticks on Shrove Tuesday" (*OED*).
25. *palt*] blow, stroke.

Nor cluck the squires that use to pip about her,
No full-blown blockhead bloated like an ox
Traverse the pit with "Damn me, what a pox."
Know then for ev'ry misdemeanor here
I'll be more stabbing, sharp, and more severe,   35
Than the fell-she that on her keeper comes,
Who in his drink last night laid waste her rooms,
Thundered her china, damned her quality,
Her glasses broke, and tore her point venie,
That dragged her by the hair, and broke her head,   40
A chamber lion, but a lamb in bed.
Like her I'll tease you for your midnight storming,
For your all talking and your no performing.
    You that with monstrous judgment force the stage,
    You fribbling, fumbling keepers of the age.   45

36. Than] *Q2, C1–3*; Then *Q1*.   43. no] *Q1, C1–3*; not *Q2*.

---

39. *point venie*] lace from Venice (or an imitation of it).

Appendix

Chronology

Approximate dates are indicated by *, occurrences in doubt by (?). Dates for plays are those on which they were first made public, either on stage or in print.

Political and Literary Events	Life and Works of Nathaniel Lee

1631
Death of Donne.
John Dryden born.

1633
Samuel Pepys born.

1635
Sir George Etherege born.*

1640
Aphra Behn born.*

1641
William Wycherley born.*

1642
First Civil War began (ended 1646).
Theaters closed by Parliament.
Thomas Shadwell born.*

1648
Second Civil War.   Born.*

1649
Execution of Charles I.

1650
Jeremy Collier born.

1651
Hobbes' *Leviathan* published.

1652
First Dutch War began (ended 1654).
Thomas Otway born.

1656
D'Avenant's *THE SIEGE OF RHODES* performed at Rutland House.

1657
John Dennis born.

1658
Death of Oliver Cromwell. D'Avenant's *THE CRUELTY OF THE SPANIARDS IN PERU* performed at the Cockpit.

Nominated to Charterhouse on May 20.

1660
Restoration of Charles II.
Theatrical patents granted to Thomas Killigrew and Sir William D'Avenant, authorizing them to form, respectively, the King's and the Duke of York's Companies.
Pepys began his diary.

1661
Cowley's *THE CUTTER OF COLEMAN STREET*.
D'Avenant's *THE SIEGE OF RHODES* (expanded to two parts).

1662
Charter granted to the Royal Society.

1663
Dryden's *THE WILD GALLANT*.
Tuke's *THE ADVENTURES OF FIVE HOURS*.

1664
Sir John Vanbrugh born.
Dryden's *THE RIVAL LADIES*.
Dryden and Howard's *THE INDIAN QUEEN*.
Etherege's *THE COMICAL REVENGE*.

1665
Second Dutch War began (ended 1667).

Entered Trinity College, Cambridge, on July 7.

Great Plague.
Dryden's *THE INDIAN EM-PEROR*.
Orrery's *MUSTAPHA*.

1666
Fire of London.
Death of James Shirley.

1667
Jonathan Swift born.
Milton's *Paradise Lost* published.
Sprat's *The History of the Royal Society* published.
Dryden's *SECRET LOVE*.

1668
Death of D'Avenant.
Dryden made Poet Laureate.
Dryden's *An Essay of Dramatic Poesy* published.
Shadwell's *THE SULLEN LOVERS*.

1669
Pepys terminated his diary.   B.A. from Cambridge.
Susannah Centlivre born.

1670
William Congreve born.
Dryden's *THE CONQUEST OF GRANADA*, Part I.

1671
Dorset Garden Theatre (Duke's Company) opened.
Colley Cibber born.
Milton's *Paradise Regained* and *Samson Agonistes* published.
Dryden's *THE CONQUEST OF GRANADA*, Part II.
THE REHEARSAL, by the Duke of Buckingham and others.
Wycherley's *LOVE IN A WOOD*.

1672
Third Dutch War began (ended   Actor in the Duke's Company.
1674).
Joseph Addison born.
Richard Steele born.

–99–

Dryden's *MARRIAGE À LA MODE.*

1674

New Drury Lane Theatre (King's Company) opened.

Death of Milton.

Nicholas Rowe born.

Thomas Rymer's *Reflections on Aristotle's Treatise of Poesy* (translation of Rapin) published.

1675

Dryden's *AURENG-ZEBE.*

Wycherley's *THE COUNTRY WIFE.**

1676

Etherege's *THE MAN OF MODE.*

Otway's *DON CARLOS.*

Shadwell's *THE VIRTUOSO.*

Wycherley's *THE PLAIN DEALER.*

1677

Aphra Behn's *THE ROVER.*

Rymer's *Tragedies of the Last Age Considered* published.

Dryden's *ALL FOR LOVE.*

1678

Popish Plot.

George Farquhar born.

Bunyan's *Pilgrim's Progress* (Part I) published.

1679

Exclusion Bill introduced.

Death of Thomas Hobbes.

Death of Roger Boyle, Earl of Orrery.

Charles Johnson born.

1680

Death of Samuel Butler.

Death of John Wilmot, Earl of Rochester.

Dryden's *THE SPANISH FRIAR.*

Otway's *THE ORPHAN.*

THE TRAGEDY OF NERO, EMPEROR OF ROME produced in May at Drury Lane.

SOPHONISBA, OR HANNIBAL'S OVERTHROW produced in April at Drury Lane.

GLORIANA, OR THE COURT OF AUGUSTUS CAESAR produced in January at Drury Lane.

THE RIVAL QUEENS, OR THE DEATH OF ALEXANDER THE GREAT produced in March at Drury Lane.

MITHRIDATES, KING OF PONTUS produced in March* at Drury Lane; *OEDIPUS* (in collaboration with Dryden) produced in November* at Dorset Garden.

CAESAR BORGIA: THE SON OF POPE ALEXANDER THE SIXTH produced in September* at Dorset Garden.

THE PRINCESS OF CLEVE produced* at Dorset Garden; *THEODOSIUS; OR, THE FORCE OF LOVE* produced in September* at Dorset Garden; *LUCIUS JUNIUS*

BRUTUS produced in December at Dorset Garden.

1681

Charles II dissolved Parliament at Oxford.

Dryden's *Absalom and Achitophel* published.

Tate's adaptation of *KING LEAR*.

1682

The King's and the Duke of York's Companies merged into the United Company.

Dryden's *The Medal*, *MacFlecknoe*, and *Religio Laici* published.

Otway's *VENICE PRESERVED*.

THE DUKE OF GUISE (in collaboration with Dryden) produced in November at Drury Lane.

1683

Rye House Plot.

Death of Thomas Killigrew.

Crowne's *CITY POLITIQUES*.

CONSTANTINE THE GREAT produced* at Drury Lane.

1684

Committed to Bedlam Hospital on November 11.

1685

Death of Charles II; accession of James II.

Revocation of the Edict of Nantes.

The Duke of Monmouth's Rebellion.

Death of Otway.

John Gay born.

Crowne's *SIR COURTLY NICE*.

Dryden's *ALBION AND AL-BANIUS*.

1687

Death of the Duke of Buckingham.

Dryden's *The Hind and the Panther* published.

Newton's *Principia* published.

1688

The Revolution.

Alexander Pope born.

Shadwell's *THE SQUIRE OF ALSATIA*.

Released from Bedlam on April 11.

1689

The War of the League of Augsburg began (ended 1697).

Toleration Act.

Death of Aphra Behn.

Shadwell made Poet Laureate.

Dryden's *DON SEBASTIAN.*

Shadwell's *BURY FAIR.*

THE MASSACRE OF PARIS (written about 1678 and suppressed by the authorities) produced November 7 at Drury Lane.

1690

Battle of the Boyne.

Locke's *Two Treatises of Government* and *An Essay Concerning Human Understanding* published.

1691

Death of Etherege.*

Langbaine's *An Account of the English Dramatic Poets* published.

1692

Death of Shadwell.

Tate made Poet Laureate.

Death in May.

1693

George Lillo born.*

Rymer's *A Short View of Tragedy* published.

Congreve's *THE OLD BACHELOR.*

1694

Death of Queen Mary.

Southerne's *THE FATAL MAR-RIAGE.*

1695

Group of actors led by Thomas Betterton left Drury Lane and established a new company at Lincoln's Inn Fields.

Congreve's *LOVE FOR LOVE.*

Southerne's *OROONOKO.*

1696

Cibber's *LOVE'S LAST SHIFT.*

Vanbrugh's *THE RELAPSE.*

1697

Treaty of Ryswick ended the War of the League of Augsburg.

Charles Macklin born.
Congreve's *THE MOURNING BRIDE*.
Vanbrugh's *THE PROVOKED WIFE*.

1698
Collier controversy started with the publication of *A Short View of the Immorality and Profaneness of the English Stage*.

1699
Farquhar's *THE CONSTANT COUPLE*.

1700
Death of Dryden.
Blackmore's *Satire against Wit* published.
Congreve's *THE WAY OF THE WORLD*.

1701
Act of Settlement.
War of the Spanish Succession began (ended 1713).
Death of James II.
Rowe's *TAMERLANE*.
Steele's *THE FUNERAL*.

1702
Death of William III; accession of Anne.
The Daily Courant began publication.
Cibber's *SHE WOULD AND SHE WOULD NOT*.

1703
Death of Samuel Pepys.
Rowe's *THE FAIR PENITENT*.

1704
Capture of Gibraltar; Battle of Blenheim.
Defoe's *The Review* began publication (1704–1713).
Swift's *A Tale of a Tub* and *The Battle of the Books* published.

Cibber's *THE CARELESS HUS-BAND*.

1705

Haymarket Theatre opened.

Steele's *THE TENDER HUS-BAND*.

1706

Battle of Ramillies.

Farquhar's *THE RECRUITING OFFICER*.

1707

Union of Scotland and England.

Death of Farquhar.

Henry Fielding born.

Farquhar's *THE BEAUX' STRATAGEM*.

1708

Downes' *Roscius Anglicanus* published.

1709

Samuel Johnson born.

Rowe's edition of Shakespeare published.

The Tatler began publication (1709–1711).

Centlivre's *THE BUSY BODY*.

1711

Shaftesbury's *Characteristics* published.

The Spectator began publication (1711–1712).

Pope's *An Essay on Criticism* published.

1713

Treaty of Utrecht ended the War of the Spanish Succession.

Addison's *CATO*.

1714

Death of Anne; accession of George I.

Steele became Governor of Drury Lane.

John Rich assumed management of
Lincoln's Inn Fields.
Centlivre's *THE WONDER: A
WOMAN KEEPS A SECRET.*
Rowe's *JANE SHORE.*

1715
Jacobite Rebellion.
Death of Tate.
Rowe made Poet Laureate.
Death of Wycherley.

1716
Addison's *THE DRUMMER.*

1717
David Garrick born.
Cibber's *THE NON-JUROR.*
Gay, Pope, and Arbuthnot's
*THREE HOURS AFTER MAR-
RIAGE.*

1718
Death of Rowe.
Centlivre's *A BOLD STROKE FOR
A WIFE.*

1719
Death of Addison.
Defoe's *Robinson Crusoe* published.
Young's *BUSIRIS, KING OF
EGYPT.*

1720
South Sea Bubble.
Samuel Foote born.
Steele suspended from the Gover-
norship of Drury Lane (restored
1721).
Little Theatre in the Haymarket
opened.
Steele's *The Theatre* (periodical)
published.
Hughes' *THE SIEGE OF
DAMASCUS.*

1721
Walpole became first Minister.

1722

Steele's *THE CONSCIOUS LOVERS.*

1723

Death of Susannah Centlivre.

Death of D'Urfey.

1725

Pope's edition of Shakespeare published.

1726

Death of Jeremy Collier.

Death of Vanbrugh.

Law's *Unlawfulness of Stage Entertainments* published.

Swift's *Gulliver's Travels* published.

1727

Death of George I; accession of George II.

Death of Sir Isaac Newton.

Arthur Murphy born.

1728

Pope's *The Dunciad* (first version) published.

Cibber's *THE PROVOKED HUSBAND* (expansion of Vanbrugh's fragment *A JOURNEY TO LONDON*).

Gay's *THE BEGGAR'S OPERA.*

1729

Goodman's Fields Theatre opened.

Death of Congreve.

Death of Steele.

Edmund Burke born.

1730

Cibber made Poet Laureate.

Oliver Goldsmith born.

Thomson's *The Seasons* published.

Fielding's *THE AUTHOR'S FARCE.*

Fielding's *TOM THUMB* (revised as *THE TRAGEDY OF TRAGEDIES*, 1731).

1731

Death of Defoe.

Fielding's *THE GRUB-STREET OPERA*.

Lillo's *THE LONDON MER-CHANT*.

1732

Covent Garden Theatre opened.

Death of Gay.

George Colman the elder born.

Fielding's *THE COVENT GAR-DEN TRAGEDY*.

Fielding's *THE MODERN HUS-BAND*.

Charles Johnson's *CAELIA*.

1733

Pope's *An Essay on Man* (Epistles I–III) published (Epistle IV, 1734).

1734

Death of Dennis.

The Prompter began publication (1734–1736).

Theobald's edition of Shakespeare published.

Fielding's *DON QUIXOTE IN ENGLAND*.

1736

Fielding led the "Great Mogul's Company of Comedians" at the Little Theatre in the Haymarket (1736–1737).

Fielding's *PASQUIN*.

Lillo's *FATAL CURIOSITY*.

1737

The Stage Licensing Act.

Dodsley's *THE KING AND THE MILLER OF MANSFIELD*.

Fielding's *THE HISTORICAL REGISTER FOR THE YEAR 1736*.